Robinson Township Library
Robinson, Illinois 62454

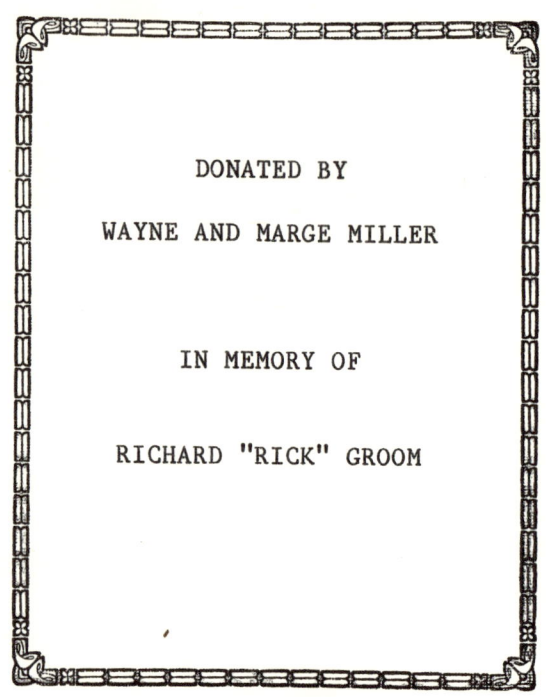

Motorcycle Books

a critical survey and checklist

by
KIRBY CONGDON

Robinson Township Library
Robinson, Illinois 62454

The Scarecrow Press, Inc.
Metuchen, N.J., & London
1987

Library of Congress Cataloging-in-Publication Data

Congdon, Kirby.
  Motorcycle books.

  1. Motorcycles--Bibliography. I. Title.
Z5173.M58C66 1987 [TL440]   016.6292'275   87-1641
ISBN 0-8108-1985-6

Copyright © 1987 by Kirby Congdon

Manufactured in the United States of America

ACKNOWLEDGEMENTS

The Science and Technology Division of

The New York Public Library

and

all the Libraries, Book Stores, and

Motorcycle Shops whose employees

gave their time and interest to my inquiries.

CONTENTS

Foreword   vii

PART I: Major Titles, Annotated   1

PART II: Comprehensive Lists, by Topic   61

      Biography   61
      Children's Books   62
      General Literature   63
      History   64
      Manufacturers   72
      Mechanics   82
      Racing   88
      Reference   93
      Restoration   94
      Riding   94
      Travel and Touring   97
      Video   97

PART III: Supplementary List by Make   101

About the Compiler   136

FOREWORD

Some twenty years ago, when I got the idea for a bibliography of motorcycle books, the literature was so limited that the subject could have been covered in a brief magazine article. The New York Public Library had one title on engines, which only happened by chance to include motorcycle engines, dated 1918. There was nothing else. Today, the flood of materials is almost beyond the scope of the individual collector's or librarian's available space and attention, if not indeed beyond their means. Given this fact, I have tried to provide here a representative selection for a basic library even though the publishing industry strives to out-date, and make obsolete, older books by up-dated replacements intended to capture the current market. While the first appeal of such a survey is to the aficionado, as inexplicable as such appeals always are, my very close second aim is to provide a broad picture for the sociologist or historian that may give some depth of understanding to the phenomenon of motorcycling as an industry, as a sport, and as a tradition.

Having been invented some one hundred years ago (1885), motorcycles are hardly new, but as an industry and sport, the general mass interest and its growth have been witnessed from their infancy, comparatively speaking, by anyone over 30. Even younger people may be able to note where there had been one motorcycle in their neighborhood, there are now several more on their block. As for tradition, it has been my contention elsewhere that the motorcycle is a transmogrification, as it were, of the American myth of the individual versus the anonymous crowd. While motorcycles have a worldwide distribution, still its appeal here in the United States fits easily into the myth we treasure of the cowboy and his horse. Even the vocabulary (the mount, the saddle, the pillion, not to overlook horsepower itself) is borrowed from equestrian times.

What one can make of this, beyond the poetic reference, I am not qualified to predict or proscribe, but I have felt a personal need to make some documentation of the phenomenon itself and my pleasure in doing so must, by way of explanation, join the explanation, as I say, for any aficionado: the interest and affection are inexplicable.

                                            Kirby Congdon
                                            Fire Island Pines

Part I

MAJOR TITLES

Contents of each book are reviewed with descriptions of the general layout, including typography, pictures, design, and writing.

Format of Entries

The entries begin with the name of the author, last name first, followed by the book's title and the physical description and bibliographic facts. These usually include: the breadth and height in centimeters and in inches; "dj" for dust jacket, if any; "cloth" or "boards" to indicate hard cover binding and "ppw" for printed paper wrapper; number of pages (excluding blank pages); "index," if any; "illus" if illustrated; place of publication, publisher, and date of publication.

1. ALTH, MAX. All About Motorcycles. Selection, Care, Repair and Safety. 14.5 x 22 cm (5½ x 8½") dj cloth, 209p illus index. New York: Hawthorn Books, 1975.

   The emphasis in this book is on maintenance and trouble-shooting for the cyclist who does not have a machine shop but who expects to do everything else for his bike short of dismantling the motor. The explanations are detailed and clear to the layman and do not assume prior mechanical knowledge or experience. The numerous mechanical line drawings are simplified. The index provides direct access to specific areas of information. The author's previous books are about bicycles, cars, locks and plumbing and this experience and background is proven in the organization and easy communication here in both a mechanical and literary sense throughout the book.

2. _____. Motorcycles and Motorcycling. 18.5 x 22 cm (7½ x 9") illus bds 90p illus, index. New York, London, Toronto: Franklin Watts, 1979.

This history traces the motorcycle back to the pedalless, gearless, steerless "celerifere" of 1791, through the pedalled gears of 1879, and also back to the external-combustion engine of the steam-driven tricycle of the early 19th century. The author documents the development of the internal-combustion gasoline engine on the primitive motorcycle from Daimler's 1885 invention, through the commercial success of this application of the gasoline engine to the bicycle in 1892 at Munich, to, finally, the 1903-04 motorcycle as such (i.e., without bicycle parts).

The following chapters explain the operation and inner workings, kinds of bikes, mopeds, and scooters, and the variety of uses (police, military, transportation, racing and its own forms of competition).

The book is simple, direct, and very well done. It is only the level of the language that relegates this beginners' book to the juvenile or children's category. Many an adult would find its contents educational and enlightening. The book could only be improved by the replacement of the black-and-white illustrations with some in color.

3. ARCTANDER, ERIK. The New Book of Motorcycles. 16.9 x 23.5 cm (6½ x 9¼") ppw 112p illus. Greenwich, CT: Fawcett Pub., 1968.

Several authors contribute articles to this anthology covering American and British antiques, current models, side cars, engines, dealers, tours, organizations, racing, and the testing of used motorcycles.

4. ARMAN, MICHAEL P. How To Buy (or Sell) A Used Motorcycle and Not Get Burned--Maybe. 15 x 23 cm (8 x 9") ppw 72p illus. Tucson, AZ: AXTEX Corp., 1979.

In a sprightly writing style, the author highly recommends used bikes and is blunt about which ones not to buy. Advice on securing titles to the vehicle is followed by detailed information on engine and frame numbering systems for the BSA, BMW, Harley-Davidson, Honda, Kawasaki, Norton Commando, Suzuki, Triumph and Yamaha. Ten pages consist of a knowledgeable checklist. Bikes which have been stored and those which have been damaged by accidents are discussed. Financing and payment procedures are given a cautionary review, along with the ins and outs of insurance, how to prevent theft, basic procedures (measuring systems, handling parts, and various ground rules) for any repair or other work, finally closing with advice for selling a bike which is as meticulous as the earlier advice for buying one.

Even if the reader is not interested in either the prospect of buying or selling a used bike, the book is excellent in providing new insights for both neophyte and "old hand," if only to confirm and verify what one had thought before was probably true.

Three or four of the 15 illustrations do not seem to have any reference to the text, and all are erratically positioned in the book.

5. AYTON, C.J. The Great Japanese Motorcycles. 22 x 28.7 cm (9-5/8 x 11¼") dj cloth 188p illus. New York: Galahad Books, 1981.

The book benefits from the limitation of the subject--Honda, Suzuki, Yamaha and Kawasaki motorcycles--with a couple of chapters on the Bridgestone and Marusho Lilac. Personal opinions, description, and racing and manufacturing history are pertinently illustrated with 151 black and white and 51 colored photographs.

6. BISHOP, GEORGE. The Encyclopedia of Motorcycling. 23.3 x 30.3 cm (9¼ x 12") ppw 192p illus. New York: Putnam, 1980.

Only 114 pages comprise the encyclopedia; the rest of the book consists of two sections: a 34-page history and 19 pages on customizing and mechanics. The encyclopedia section is an alphabetical list confined almost entirely to brands and riders. An eleven-page glossary in the back of the book defines the specialized vocabulary. There are many illustrations and 40 pages are in color. The editorial slant, however, seems to be toward the British locale, where the book was originally produced.

7. BOSWELL, CLIFF and GEORGE HAYS. Two-Wheel Touring & Camping. 21.5 x 29 cm (8½ x 11-3/4") ppw 86p illus. Sierra Madre, CA: Bagnall Publishing Co., 1969.

The authors cover preparation, equipment, recreational areas, maps and how to get them, general planning, camping, international travel in a section "across the borders," and advice on photography.

The enumeration of many items of know-how proves the experience of the writers, and these tips are reminders of all those commonsense things you "just happened to forget about" when you're 30 miles down the road. The text is always pertinent--no verbiage to fill up a page--and the numerous illustrations include tips on packing and camping. There are a lot of scenic shots with the inevitable bike in the foreground--as a last insidious persuasion for the reader to hit the road.

8. BROKAW, PAUL M. A Study of the Four-Stroke Motorcycle Engine. 21.5 x 28 cm (8½ x 11") ppw 63p, 33 illus. Sierra Madre, CA: Bagnall Publishing Co., 1970.

While a lucidly written description of the four-stroke cycle opens the book, an abbreviation, TDC (on page 1) and later, BDC, are never defined unless one has read as far as page 8 and notices an illustration that happens to have the words Top Dead Center spelled out in it. The book is otherwise a meticulous and clear introduction to four-stroke cycle engines, carburetors and their types, and other engine components. Chapter Nine covers roadside engine failures followed with two supplements, one on conversions to the metric system and an exam on the book. A sub-title on the jacket reads, "Introduction to practical engineering written in the language and interests of the mechanic" but the book is recommended for any level of interest for all motorcyclists, mechanically inclined or not.

The illustrations consist of technical drawings which balance the text.

9. BURRIS, ROD. Velocette, A Development History of

the MSS, Venom, Viper, Thruxton and Scrambler Models. 17.3 x 23.2 cm (6-3/4 x 9") paperback 160p index. Sparkford (England): Haynes Publishing Group, 1982.

A German immigrant to England, aged 19, marketed the first "Veloce" fifteen years later in 1905. The entire period is passed over with the phrase, "He became involved in the manufacture of cycles and after taking over Isaac Taylor and Company, formed a new firm under the name of John Taylor." There is no further information on the man or the company for these crucial years, although the subsequent evolution of the Velocette is given in some detail in regard to how 75-mph machines of 500cc came about by the middle 1930's. To this extent, the book lives up to its title. Always a good-looking machine--according to the approximately 130 photographs of bikes in the book--the lack of demand and, later, production assembly problems both created trouble in 1948, as the BSA and Matchless gained favor by purchasers in the British military.

Sales representatives in California encouraged the production of the 500 for the American market and Scramblers were manufactured as well through the 1950's, making such names as the Clubman and Venom (500cc) and the Viper (350cc) familiar to Americans, as well as the Thruxton engine.

10. CADDELL, LAURIE and MIKE WINFIELD. The Book of Superbikes. 21.5 x 27.7 cm (8½ x 11") ppw 160p illus index. Tucson, AZ: H.P. Books, 1981.

The book provides a handsome survey, mostly of the past two decades, of 44 big bikes in 157 close-ups and portraits, all in color. A descriptive write-up deals with distinctive features, history, and operation. Individual specifications are entered separately. While the book is a "small quarto" in size, page breaks distort the appearance and proportions of many of the full-length profiles of machines. The coverage on older machines includes the Vincent Black Shadow (1952), Zundapp K80 (1933), Ariel Square Four (1930), Matchless Silver Hawk (1930), Scott Flying Squirrel (1925), Coventry Eagle (1922), Brough Superior (1925), Cleveland Four (1925-30), Ace Four (1920), Indian Big Chief (1920-28), Henderson Four (1913-28), and two very early bikes: the Excelsior Series 61 (1912) and the FN Four (1905).

11. _____ and JASPER SPENCER-SMITH. Modern Motor Bikes in Colour. 14 x 20 cm (5½ x 8") dj cloth 153p illus. Dorset (England): Blandford Press, 1979.

Seventy-four numbered colored photographs by Spencer-Smith are well presented in alphabetical order and are accompanied in a separate section by corresponding descriptions which are brief but knowledgeable.

Caddell's introduction speculates on the appeal to the general public of various innovations from the small moped to the big road-runners.

Brands included are Benelli, BMW, Bimota, Cossack, CZ, CKW, Ducati, Fantic, Harley-Davidson, Honda, India, Kawasaki, Laverda, Morini, Moto Meriden, Moto Guzzi, MV Augusta, MZ, Norton, Quasar, Rickman, Royal Enfield, Seeley, Suzuki, Silk, Triumph, and Yamaha.

12. _____. Powerbikes. 19.7 x 25.5 cm (8 x 10") dj cloth 160p illus index. Poole, Dorset (England): Blandford Press, 1981.

Thirty bikes are selected to represent "the fastest roadsters, the most powerful mudpluggers, and the swiftest racers" available in the late 1970's. These are as follows:

Honda MT125R	Ducati 900SS
Kawasaki KR250/350	Bimota SB3
Suzuki SP370	BMW R100RS
Honda XL500S	Harley-Davidson XLCR-1000
Suzuki RG500	Honda GL1000 Gold Wing
Yamaha XT500	Honda RCB Endurance Racer
Silk 700S	
Seeley Honda 750	Kawasaki Z1000ST
Triumph Bonneville	Laverda Jota
Yamaha TX750	Rickman Endurance
Moto Guzzi Le Mans	Suzuki GS1000S
MV-Agusta Monza	Van Veen OCR1000
Norton Commando	Honda CBX
Quasar	Yamaha SX1100
Benelli 900	Kawasaki Z1300
	Munch Mammut

13. CARRICK, PETER. The Book of Motor Cycle Racing. 15 x 23.5 cm (6 x 9¼") dj bds 126p illus. London: Stanley Paul, 1967.

 While covering the British scene, the book covers universal subjects in such chapters as "How to Break into Racing," "Look After Your Machines" (on tuning), and "Winning a Big Race," as well as commentary on and by racers. One brief chapter is on broadcasting and camera work. Photographs depict individuals racing and in related situations "off-camera." Champions of 1965-66 are listed.

14. _____. Encyclopedia of Motor-Cycle Sport. 16 x 24 cm (6¼ x 9½") dj cloth 224p illus. New York: St. Martin's, 1977.

 The illustrations consist of two groups of portraits of riders, but the book is not an illustrated encyclopedia as such. The information is confined mostly to riders, racing, winners, and records. There are no items referring to mechanical nomenclature or technical statistics outside of the title's reference to involvement in the sport itself.

15. _____. The Guinness Guide to Motorcycling. 21 x 29.5 cm (8¼ x 11-3/4") dj cloth 223 p illus index. Enfield, Middlesex (England): Guinness Superlatives Limited, 1980.

 This guide attempts to "have conveyed something of the excitement, satisfaction, glamour, romance, skills and thrills of motorcycling yesterday and today." The opening chapter covers early manufacturing history. The second chapter takes up the beginning of racing in the first decades of this century in England. Beginners' advice is interjected before an account of international manufacturing booms and busts, technological changes and general surveys of racing in 60 pages. Separate chapters are on the Isle of Man Tourist Trophy races, off-road riding, motocross, trials/enduros, grass track/ice/sand, speedway, speed records, sprints/drag races, and marathons. The latter half of the book covers famous riders, factories, world titles, and championships.
 Captions are in bold 6-point type whereas 8-point

would have been a better accompaniment to the text. There are many illustrations, 193 being in black and white and 37 in color.

16. _____. Superbikes. Road-burners to Record-Breakers. 24.7 x 31 cm (9-3/4 x 12") dj cloth 80p illus index. London: Octopus Books, 1982.

    Besides classic stock road bikes of contemporary times and of previous years, exotic choppers from private garages, off-road and on-road racers as well as dragsters are represented in a panoply of 73 professional color portraits.

17. CHARTWELL BOOKS INC. Motorcycle & Moped Maintenance. 22.5 x 29.5 cm (8-3/4 x 11½") dj bds 89p. Secaucus, NJ: Chartwell Books Inc., 1978.

    While this bibliography excludes most technical reference books, this one is included because of its thorough attention to ordinary maintenance. The book opens with descriptions of types of machines, how to test second-hand bikes and basic tools, and it ends with sophisticated electrical fault-finding. Well-illustrated with drawings and black and white photographs to supplement the text.

18. CHRISTENSEN, RICHARD D. Motorcycles in Magazines 1895-1983. 14.5 x 22 cm (5-3/4 x 8-3/4") cloth 342p illus. Metuchen, NJ: Scarecrow Press, 1985.

    Every motorcyclist has been curious about the test runs and "reviews" given his machine by writers and by the staff on magazines when his model first appeared. Almost invariably, however, that particular issue of the publication appeared long before one has bought one's bike and there is no clue as to which magazine the write-up was in if there was a write-up in the first place. This book answers that need to find such information.
    An index to the motorcycles themselves refers the reader to its literary coverage in the chronologically ordered list of magazines beginning with the early years of the motorcycle's invention, 1895. These early entries are a <u>tour de force</u> in regard to the research required.

While the book may seem specialized, it is essential to any library that serves general community needs.

Nine drawings illustrate representative motorcycle designs "selected for the richness of its character."

Our only fault with the book is the flat-looking type face, which is reduced typewriter copy.

19. CLAMPETT, BOB. The Motorcycle Handbook. 10½ x 17-3/4 cm (4 x 7") ppw 240p illus index. Greenwich, CT: Fawcett Publications, 1975.

Designed to be read selectively, individual sections cover history, sizes, brands and models, construction, purchase, learning to ride--technique and safety, dirt riding, equipment with a list of 121 manufacturers' names (but no addresses or identification of their product), advanced riding and racing, maintenance and legalities. Names and addresses of motorcycle manufacturers and of periodicals close the book, which is indexed.

20. CLIFFORD, PETER. The Art and Science of Motor Cycle Road Racing. 17.5 x 24.5 cm (7 x 9½") dj cloth 268p. Richmond, Surrey (England): Hazleton Publishing Co., 1982.

Kenny Roberts, in his introduction, says flat out that there is no art to racing; it is all science. But then he details how an artist works!--by search, by analysis, study, and planning, much as an architect or sculptor works; that is, the area between the inspiration and the achievement is, as always, part desire and part recipe. And who can really separate them? Perhaps the difference between sport and art is that one is competitive--against others--and the other is non-competitive and _for_ others. But the process of dedication is the same and that kind of concern is what this book undertakes to describe and lay out.

The first real comment (by Barry Sheene) on racing is one that is very understandable to the outsider: "... at the age of seventeen Ron Chandler came blasting past me on a 500 and I thought 'Jeez, this has got to be the worst thing in the world!'" Danger, risk, age and experience are frankly discussed. The phenomenon of man coping "naturally" with the complexities of physics in cornering and in the aerodynamics is explained in theory and practice. A chapter surveys the rules and regulations for the races, the machines, gear worn by the rider and prize money. Engineering design is discussed in regard to cylinders, exhaust pipes, pistons, frames, steering assemblies, braking, and suspensions.

While pertinent footnotes attempt to clear up sometimes baffling terms, the information is a little specialized for the layman reader who has had no real shop experience or mechanical instincts, but this section of the book removes a lot of mystery if not the complexity of engineering.

Tires (invented in 1888, by the way) get their own contemporary treatment in a complete chapter.

The nearest airport and town and the length of the track are included with a racer's description for each of 22 maps of major world racing circuits. Some bird's-eye-view drawings are also borrowed from the 1982 issue of the annual, Motocourse, another Hazleton Publishing book, edited by the author.

Only 44 pages toward the end of the book deal with the technique of racing as such and the promise of the book's title may seem exaggerated to some readers. The book is more a "primer" on the background of racing than it is any kind of professional or even amateur racer's guide. As the author admits, "most riders do not consider it knowledge that can be passed on ... or ... readily put into words." However, he encapsulates the techniques of starting, slipstreaming, braking, cornering, pre-race practice, gear changes, carburetors, tires and suspension. One chapter, "Race Day," considers the psychological aspects before and after racing, pointing out that the man who finishes fourteenth may achieve great satisfaction, knowing he has improved his technique and done well, while the man who came in second may be only depressed.

In the chapter, "Rivals," 25 miniature biographies cover prominent racers.

The rigors of travel--customs, expenses, distance-- are brought up for European circuits. The book closes with a few comments on retirement.

The book is handsomely produced, proofread and set in a legible typeface. Ninety-eight black-and-white illustrations and 18 mostly full-page color photographs, with some 23 engineering graphics, accompany the text.

21. _____, editor. Motocourse 1982-83. 24 x 32 cm (9½ x 12½") dj bds 192p illus. Richmond, Surrey (England): Hazleton, 1982.

The format of this book is that of a magazine in that this is the seventh annual publication and 26 pages of this issue consist of advertisements. No expense seems to have been spared in regard to its production, photography, writing and research on the motorcycle road racing "season." Racing statistics, tables, graphic maps, specifications, and reportage abound. Photographs with biographical information on the top ten world champions are an opening feature with extensive articles on racing in Argentina, Austria, France, Spain, Italy (Misano Adriatico, and San Marino), Holland, Belgium, Yugoslavia, Britain (and Isle of Man), Sweden, Finland, Czechoslovakia, and Germany.

Specific events in the United States are not covered except for a listing of the results of 17 competitions for 1982.

22. _____. Motocourse. 24 x 32 cm (9½ x 13") dj cloth 192p. Richmond, Surrey (England): Hazleton Publishing, 1986.

This edition of the annual includes a chapter on the retired (1984) Barry Sheene, and articles by various writers on technical experimentation on the Suzuki Skoal Bandit, improvements for financial incentives, specifications for 500cc racing which are discussed and listed for four bikes, each in the 500, 125, 80 cc. endurance and sidecar classes. The particular competitive distinction for these is not given, although, ostensibly, this may be looked up in the extensive list that follows of Grand Prix winners covering 1949-85. The controversy over track safety on major race tracks in 12 countries is brought up with a composite evaluation of each by unidentified "regular Grand Prix riders throughout the season." A very thorough report covers these same 12 world championship rounds for 1985 in a separately indexed section from page 66 to page 151. Special feature articles on places (racing in the southern hemisphere, Dunlop Island in the Irish Sea, and the Isle of Man) and on particular riders' performances and their machines. These are covered in detail by nine writers.

Racing results from 14 meets in Great Britain, Italy,

Austria, Northern Ireland, and the Isle of Man, with 20 competitions under the United States road racing category are listed, concluding the last nine pages of the book.

The coverage on the top ten riders for 1985 include Freddie Spencer (United States), Eddie Lawson, Carlos Lavado, Wayne Gardner, Toni Mang, Martin Wimmer, Ron Haslam, Randy Mamola, Christian Sarron and Loris Reggiani.

While packed with information, the text is printed in a very small point size that seems out of keeping with such an otherwise elaborate book with its 54 color and 144 black and white illustrations, good paper and nicely done layout. Even the advertisers, who are given space in magazine style, seem to have gone all out with distinctive, full-page color ads to make an impression in this ultimate history and reference volume.

23. CLYMER, FLOYD. A Treasury of Motorcycles of the World. 22 x 28.2 cm (8-3/4 x 11") dj bds 237p. New York: Crown Pub., 1965.

   Profusely illustrated with black-and-white photographs and graphics, the author covers the motorcycle boom in America and moves into riding, instruction, engine construction, catalogs of models, available accessories, and racing. Six pages present models from the Ford Museum in Dearborn, Michigan and the section, "Yesterday," covers aspects of advertising, movies, and commercial history in 60 pages.

24. COONFIELD, ED. Enduro Secrets Revealed. 14 x 21.8 cm (5½ x 8½") ppw 176p illus. Salida, CO: Hourglass Publishing, 1985.

   The book is nothing if not thorough. While the compiler of this bibliography is concerned more with the attraction and the lore of motorcycling, if he were to get into competition, he would relish the insights this book by Coonfield offers--such as diet before a competition, the kind of watch to look for, previous practice for hurdles--the sort of detail other writers seem to take for granted.

   The book is not printed by a nationally recognized press and the ordinary type and the over-soft reproduction of the otherwise good illustrations on an only adequate paper reflect this, unfortunately. But most much more elaborate and expensive big coffee-table books would be hard put to provide as much concern and advice to the motorcyclist interested in competition. One could say a "real" book like this distinguishes the difference between a mere observer's enthusiasm and the dedicated motorcycle-rider enthusiast, not to mention the passion of the competitor himself.

25. CRAVEN, KEN. Ride It! The Complete Book of Motorcycle Touring. 21 x 27.5 cm (8¼ x 11") illus bds 134p illus. Sparkford (England): The Haynes Publishing Group, 1977.

Engagingly written, topics included are map-reading for perspective and other topographical insights; psychological and organizational advice on group touring; camping with attention to bedding, food supplies, and cooking; "house"-keeping, clothing, packing; medical advice, preventive medicine; maintenance, running economics (with remarks on expenses in Europe); orientation while traveling; physical fitness; foreign languages; mountain roads; riding tips; emergencies, and sidecars. An appendix lists heights, routes, and winter conditions of 67 European mountain passes in six countries (and one in Andorra).

The author and his wife have run over 40 organized motorcycle tours. Their experience and advice centers mostly on European references but the text considers the American reader, with interesting and pertinent graphics and 145 black-and-white photographs, mostly drawn from the author's own experiences.

26. CUTTER, ROBERT ARTHUR. The New Guide to Motorcycling. 17 x 24 cm (6-3/4 x 9½") dj cloth illus. New York: Arco Publishing Co., 1974.

The author provides thorough advice for the beginner and covers every category from purchase to riding conditions (in the night, in rain, and in the country) as well as advice on insurance, break-in period, clothing and accessories. The last chapter covers facts on the American Motorcycle Association.

The photography tends to be visually decorative

rather than instructive or necessary, but the pictures dress the book up and present familiar scenes of shop interiors and people riding and learning to ride.

27. DAVIS, PEDR. All About Motorcycles. 21 x 28 cm (8¼ x 11") bds 77p. New York: Paul Hamlyn Pty Ltd, 1974.

This book gives all the generalized information there is about motorcycles and riding with mechanical diagrams, drawings and photographs. The book concludes with brief descriptions of popular types of bikes.

28. DITCHBURN, BLACKETT. Superbiking. 18.5 x 21.3 cm (7¼ x 8¼") illus colored wrappers, 127p illus. London: Osprey Publishing Limited, 1983.

There are 91 black-and-white photographs in this book. As spoiled as we are by the plenitude of color in motorcycle books, one misses this perk but as these pictures are all of the same person on only a couple of different bikes to illustrate the text, the reader can't sulk too much. The pictures are often redundant and don't demonstrate the specific idea intended, but the photography is always pictorially pleasing and the shots are nicely cropped, although it is disconcerting to see the rider on the left side of these English roads. Backgrounds, as so often happens in this area of photographic documentation, do not detract from the handsomely leathered rider and his bike. The professional hand is consistent throughout the book in both the original photography and the editing. The book is not specifically about big bikes as such, as the title suggests; it is about riding the roads on one.

The book opens with the appealing statement that motorcycles are an emotional involvement in "the thrill of riding fast and well ... to look over the edge and yet return safely to tell the tale." The rest of the book tells us how to do it--if not look over the edge, then at least to tell the tale!

In a word, it is style--how to control your bike in the way that is most comfortable and safest for the rider. This pertains to road riding for both the beginner and the experienced. The author points out that the race track is another matter.

Major Titles / 15

While Superbiking is, in effect, merely a verbalization of what every rider already knows--the tricks of cornering, carrying passengers, the vagaries of traction--the analyses point up details even for the experienced motorcyclist. The discussions confirm, or emphasize, what we knew instinctively but which it never hurts to know better on a conscious level.

29. DRAKE, ALBERT. Riding Bike in the 'Fifties. 18 x 21.5 cm (7 x 8½") ppw illus unpaged (20)p illus. Okemos, MI: Stone Press, 1973.

Softly lit photographs of the period illustrate this prose poem that documents the sport of motorcycle lore before the sport became fashionable. Sections are broken down into The Morning Speed Run, Who Rode, What We Rode, Sensations, What We Hated, What We Loved, On Seeing The Wild One, and On Being the Wild One.

30. EDUCATIONAL READING SERVICE. My Super Book of Motorcycles and Motorbikes. 19 x 26 cm (7½ x 10¼") ppw 43p illus. Mahwah, NJ: Educational Reading Service, 1971.

This children's book covers representative bikes-- one each from Spain, Italy and Germany, two from Japan, three from the United States and 11 from Great Britain. The illustrations, each of which covers two pages, are artist's renditions in color. A brief paragraph of description is accompanied by a line-drawing profile, and the statistics for the size of the engine, maximum speed and the number of gear positions are listed.

31. ENGEL, LYLE KENYON and text by DEKE HOULGATE. The Complete Motorcycle Book. 16.5 x 24 cm (6½ x 9¼") dj bds 195p illus, index. New York: Four Winds Press, 1974.

This press is a division of Scholastic Magazines and is printed with the younger reader in mind: large type, well illustrated and with an introduction by Evel Knievel for prestige. The historical research on the invention and early evolution of the motorcycle is very thorough.

16 / Motorcycle Books

Safety precautions and riding instructions are emphasized with well-organized information--that is, questions on laws, riding, hazards are answered in detail with numbered paragraphs. Maintenance, various kinds of racing, and speculation about future motorcycle innovations receive separate chapters. The book concludes with names and statistics on champions, speed records, and the addresses of makers of motorcycles available in the United States. Eighty-eight black and white photographs are pertinent and interesting.

32. FORBES, MALCOLM. Around the World on Hot Air and Two Wheels. 22.5 x 29 cm (8-3/4 x 11½") dj cloth 272p illus. New York: Simon and Schuster, 1985.

  This is an anthology of articles which may have been edited by Malcolm Forbes and to which he does contribute intermittent pages of his own. The Introduction reprints an interview with him taken from <u>Playboy</u> magazine. The real authors are acknowledged at the chapter heads as Jean-Lou Colin, Gordon Cruikshanks, Dick and Donna Brown, Cook Nielson, Roger Hull, Allan Girdler, Tim Forbes, Clifford D. May and Barry Coleman (two chapters). For motorcycle enthusiasts, the book offers several chapters beyond those about ballooning. There are 449 interesting photographs in color. A few pictures show the hazards of good, bad, and indifferent roads in foreign places, with the Forbes family done up, looking rather elegant, in full black leather. One suspects that motorcycling is, for Mr. Forbes, an excuse for wearing the outfit rather than the other way around. But why not? He bears his involvement with being Mr. Forbes with more humor and good will than is given to many another rich man. You can always be a leader if you can pay for a following and to do so in a balloon or on a motorcycle seems much more sensible than to do it like, say, Hearst, with a war.
  Cook Nielson of <u>Cycle</u> magazine briefly describes the behavior of the Van Veen motorcycle on a trip by bike from London to Tangier, and Roger Hull has a 40-page chapter from <u>Road Rider</u> magazine on a specially permitted bike trip from Munich to Moscow. Allan Girdler of <u>Cycle World</u> covers a trip from Oslo to the northern end of Norway, Cape Nord, and back down via the east coast of Sweden. Malcolm Forbes' son, Tim, describes

their trips in China, and another tour through the length of Pakistan is recorded by Clifford D. May of Forbes magazine. Barry Coleman of Cycle magazine covers a trip from Alexandria, Egypt, to the Aswan dam and almost to the border of Israel by way of Suez, as well as another excursion in Thailand, Malaysia, and Brunei.

Each chapter has a map of the itinerary with innumerable pictures of the balloons flown in each city and documentary shots of the motorcycle caravans, which often include trucks, helicopters, guides, mechanics, local dignitaries, and rulers of state.

Unfortunately for motorcycle enthusiasts, the book appeared too early to include a huge motorcycle balloon first launched in June, 1986, in Normandy under Mr. Forbes' auspices.

33. FOSTER, GERALD. Cult of the Harley-Davidson. 21 x 22 cm (8¼ x 9") ppw, 128p illus. London: Osprey Publishing, Ltd., 1982.

The author seems to document the impression that motorcyclists, or at least the owners of the Harley-Davidson brand, are terrified of the English language and pride themselves in hackneyed slang and illiterate grammar. This corroborates the visual impression that such people are invariably male, over-weight, bearded, irreverent, unwashed and that they only know how to order beer at a bar. This is meant, apparently, to imply that the rest of civilization is foreign, effete, and brain-washed. The extreme defensiveness of this position is unnecessary as the motorcycle machine is one of awesome complexity, technological sophistication, and is spare and disciplined in its efficiency and function. The "mystique" of the Harley-Davidson "cult" seems quite understandable without these protective encumbrances acquired by those who seem to need an in-group togetherness to know who they themselves are. In a country founded on independence, individuality and pluralistic backgrounds, this self-abnegation is amazingly inconsistent if not somehow desperate.

Once again, an American book seems to have had to go to an English publisher to get produced. Perhaps the uncertainty about the respectability of an American image extends to business executives as well as to motorcyclists as such. Presented mostly as a handsome picture book, there are 117 color photographs (plus the covers) on high-finish paper. Restorations, custom jobs, "portraits," and documentary snap-shots are featured. And many people are clean-shaven, and look quite intelligent without the slightest suggestion of being apologetic about having their pictures taken with their Harley-Davidson motorcycles.

34. GANSBERGER, CHRISTINE. The Motorcycle Coloring Book. 28 x 21.5 cm (11 x 8½") ppw unpaged (24)p illus. Los Angeles: Price/Stern/Sloan Publishers, 1974.

   Twenty-two outlined drawings on one side of the page depict varieties of motorcycles with their riders. (One drawing is merely of a helmet.)
   Intended for children, it would make an amusing gift for a motorcycle aficionado with a sense of humor. The back cover, in color, shows the budding artist how to do it.

35. GRANT, GREGOR. AJS. The History of a Great Motorcycle. 19 x 25.5 cm (7¼ x 10") dj cloth 112p illus. London: Patrick Stephens, 1969.

   The A. J. Stevens company made their first motorcycle in 1897 and ostensibly will have a hundredth birthday. That history is covered in detail with seventy-four photographs, with supplementary drawings of engine parts.
   A list of riders, the year and finishing position in races is provided from 1911 through 1969.

36. GREENE, BOB. Motorcycle Sport Book. 21.5 x 28.2 cm (8½ x 11") dj bds 224p illus. Los Angeles: Petersen Publishing Co., 1967.

   Also produced in paper-back, this compendium is a classic survey of the basic concerns of the enthusiast: beginning, buying, construction, maintenance, and racing. It is thoroughly illustrated.

37. _____. Motorcycle Sport Book. 21.2 x 27.8 cm (8½ x 11") ppw 192p. Los Angeles: Petersen Publishing Co., 1968.

"Third annual edition," this one updates models and accessories. Various chapters cover clubs, sidecars, stunting, runs, the chassis, brakes, the Bonneville Salt Flats, and engine design.

38. GRIFFIN, AL. Motorcycles. A Buyer's & Rider's Guide. 16 x 23.5 cm (6½ x 9¼") dj cloth 317p illus index. Chicago: Henry Regnery Co., 1974.

In his opening remarks, the author gives a brief summary of manufacturing history followed by a discussion of clubs and prejudices against motorcyclists. Good cautionary advice on highway riding is provided in one chapter and page 37 to 217 describes varieties of bikes with statistics, performance, engineering, and types with definitions: superbikes, café racers, choppers, touring bikes, what the author calls day cruisers (for "outings" rather than pure touring), expressway and street bikes (for local transportation), minibikes, trail bikes for climbing, wood bikes (for overnight camping), desert bikes (cross country), and competition bikes. The book finishes with a discussion of clothing, accessories, insurance, financing, and legislation. Lists of motorcycle clubs as well as one of "outlaw motorcycle groups," speed records publications and motorcycle distributors are given.

39. GUTKIND, LEE. Bike Fever. 14.5 x 21.7 cm (8¼ x 5-3/4") dj cloth 234p. Chicago: Follett Publishing Co., 1973.

The book opens with brief notes on places, people, and experiences on a cross-country tour. This nomadic ambience of the motorcycle trip suggests the American transposition of mythology in which the adventurer becomes the hero of his own journey by overcoming physical obstacles en route to a destination even if there is no real destination to arrive at except the idea of having a round-trip journey. Even if it may be a weak fulfillment of any national mythology, the romance of the impulse is nicely documented in chapters on social, legal, manufacturing, and speed statistics and opinions on riders, racing, renegades, stuntmen, clubs, groups, purchase, and varieties of motivation and self-identification.

Unfortunately, the author closes his remarks on Evel

Knieval with the opinion that it is better to be crafty than to be a man of one's word, especially after you're rich, because others have gotten away with it without any pecuniary embarrassment. Otherwise, the author scans the romance of cycling in its many aspects with accuracy, enthusiasm, and affection, although the diction of his dramatized dialogue sounds highly improbable.

The book concludes with a frank appraisal of the ecological hazards of trail riding and suggests that this recent interest should be a permenent feature but restricted to wasteland areas. What comprises a "wasteland" is not discussed.

40. HANRAHAN, BRYAN. Bikes and Bikies. 20.5 x 28.5 cm (8¼ x 11") cloth 120p illus. Melbourne (Australia): Lansdowne Press, 1974.

Thirteen writers contribute 19 chapters to this anthology of articles on history, the Isle of Man races, the Norton, racing in Australia, Australian racers in America, trials and scrambles, motocross, Sunraysia desert rally (near Victoria), the technicalities of tire design, and, finally, an autobiographical chapter on the Australian racer, Rory Hanrahan. The book has 145 graphics and photographs, 26 of which are in color.

41. HARLEY-DAVIDSON.

In 1919 Harley-Davidson provided a "Standards of Practice" manual consisting of 410 questions and answers, "developed initially for training World War I soldiers" according to sources in David K. Wright's book on that company. This was the first piece of literature on motorcycling this reviewer is aware of-- aside from early periodicals and technical guides for repairs and maintenance. However, Harley-Davidson's house-organ, "The Enthusiast" which was briefly offered in Spanish as well as English, began in 1911 and is still in print with current issues.

42. HARRIS, MAZ. Bikers. Birth of a Modern Day Outlaw. 19 x 24.5 cm (7½ x 9-3/4") ppw 128p illus index. London & Boston: Faber and Faber, 1985.

The author explains the economic and social situations

that produced the diffident outlook and the "outsider" philosophy of motorcyclists of an anti-social sort. It seems that an introverted in-group has confused the convenience of crime with social defiance, and has confused legal disobedience with the responsibility of civil disobedience, and all of this has been wrapped up in the romance and the myth of the outlaw of the wild west. The need and the satisfaction concurrent with these thin ideas are accurately weighed by the author and are compared to similar movements in the rebellion, and finally the fashion, of the English teddy boy. The writer goes deeper for his source material on social aberration than any other author on this subject that we know of, and he manages to lift the subject above the sensational. He points out that the anti-social motivations for action were not "a search for death. It was a search for life ...." (albeit often at someone else's expense). Nor does the author miss the point of the double standard by the public in equating war with manhood, and nonconformity with degeneracy.

This kind of photographic essay from England has been better produced in the United States. A paperback, it consists of 138 random snapshots of what one might call adult children, and seems to want to weld the idea of self-indulgence or lawlessness with motorcycles and leather clothing when all three--people, clothing, and machines--may be very handsome indeed. In this book, however, the people don't seem to have all that much in the way of personality or originality and they do not come across as well as their motorcycles do. Perhaps I want my vagrants to fall into the tradition of the wandering minstrel or the wandering poet who in their defiance of social regimentation still contribute to their civilization instead of ignoring it, if not destroying it.

The author suggests there is not only misunderstanding about the "motorcycle subculture" but that this culture itself finds itself mystifying. I see no mystery myself and enjoy many of the same aspects the author does, but if anything is worth doing, it should be done well and the only mystery about that is when the doing is shallow, selfish, poorly felt, and poorly thought out. Pleasure without depth makes one a passive victim rather than an independent person that these people halfheartedly aspire to. One feels no one of these people

that are depicted here has ever done anything for any
country, for any cause larger than themselves, or for
anyone else besides themselves. Their protestations
and assertions about the sentiments of friendship, honor
and dignity before either self-imposed danger or death
are only that: mere sentimental assertions. The reader
comes away not so much with a sense of criticism but of
disappointment in a life style that professes to be free
and basic, when it is really only one of evasion and
convenience. It has nothing to do with the technological sophistication of motorcycles except as a coinciden-
tal preoccupation. The book is valuable as a proof of
the large gap between the two.

The text is "illustrated" in effect with poetry and
song lyrics, most of it pretty bad, but Albert Drake
and Thom Gunn, perhaps because they are professional
writers, survive this use of their work.

As a documentary history, the book is well done,
but as an <u>apologia pro vita sua</u> it is not very convinc-
ing because an excessive concern in a "lifestyle" with
other people's opinions and the need "to outrage the
public" do not add up to the almost religious overtones
of "a way of life."

43. HILL, RAY. Dirt Bikes. 22.5 x 23.5 cm (9 x 9") illus
bds unpaged (48)p. A Golden Wheels Book. New York:
Golden Press, 1974.

Explanations of enduro, trail, and motocross machines
are provided in the foreword. The remainder of the
book consists of 37 handsome portraits of 20 different
makes of bikes in these categories and additional action
shots and close-ups, all in color. Specifications are
given in each instance along with a few paragraphs con-
taining a brief background of the manufacturer and a
description of the particular model's construction and
performance.

44. HOLLIDAY, BOB. Motorcycle Panorama. A Pictorial
Review of Design and Development. 19.5 x 24.5 cm
(7½ x 9-3/4") dj cloth 112p illus. New York: Arco
Publishing Co., 1974.

Unusual portraits of very early motorcycle makes
distinguish this book with 29 pictures dating before

1920 and well over 50 illustrate the next three decades up to 1980. Oddly enough, only one page covers 1960 to 1969. The last dozen pages cover the early seventies. Brief histories describe 99 brands. All the photographs are in black and white. The book is a succinct answer to a librarian's inquiry about a book "that shows the main changes that have been made, from the year 1894 to the present day."

45. HOUGH, RICHARD and L.J.K. SETRIGHT. A History of the World's Motorcycles. 19 x 24.7 cm (7½ x 9-3/4") dj cloth 192p illus index. New York: Harper & Row, 1966.

   Six chapters cover ten to fifteen years of development beginning with a summary of steam and of three-wheeled experiments and concluding at 1965. Five-and-a-half pages of Chapter 2, "1901-1915 Evolution of the Fit," are anthologized in Twistgrip by Setright, along with a war anecdote from page 147.
   Well illustrated with 180 black-and-white pictures, graphics, and advertisements and with eight more in color, the illustrations accompany the text wherever pertinent.
   Brief sub-chapters cover side-car development.
   The book is oriented toward British history. (Only two well-known motorcycle brands existed in the United States after World War I in 1919 while England had 200 --to make a general comparison.) But an American interest is taken into account and one section of 25 pages covers "Fast Foreigners." However, the survey of many brands and their individual experiments and improvements in the over-all development of the motorcycle is impressive, if not astounding.

46. HOWARD, DENNIS, compiler and editor. Vintage Motor Cycle Album. 21.5 x 30.4 cm (8½ x 12") dj bds 95(1)p illus. London: Frederick Warne, 1982.

   The typography and layout are a little fustian as befits the topic perhaps but the book is all-of-a-piece and it does capture the charm and romance of earlier days, although the last chapter on the mechanics of the Honda Gold Wing is a subject that may be historical but hardly vintage.

24 / Motorcycle Books

Eighty-three photographs and 20 diagrammatic illustrations and drawings with two photographic end papers provide a visual survey of riders, bikes and events. The text covers racing days in England of Ray Abbott before World War I, "caption essays" on four nineteen-fifties bikes (Matchless, Panther, Ariel, and AJS), riding days of an Australian woman in the nineteen-twenties, a restoration shop in London, and various reminiscences on rubber boots, side cars, competitions, three chapters on the Ehrlich Motor Company (EMC) bikes (circa 1947), and finally a reminiscence of the Brough Superior (from around the 1940's).

47. JACKSON, BOB. Street Biking. How to Ride to Save Your Hide. 21.5 x 27.5 cm (8½ x 11") illus ppw 160p illus index. Tucson, AZ: H. P. Books, 1980.

As assertion of the pleasure in riding on the street (versus racing or trail-riding) opens the book. This is followed by a brief but pertinent review of different sizes to choose a first bike from, along with new and used purchase advice, insurance information and a glossary of specification terms. Separate chapters cover riding on the highway, safety in regard to clothing, traction, passengers, and state legal requirements, touring, antiques, café racers, sidecars, maintenance, tune-ups, and accessories.

The book is generally oriented toward the temperate climate. Boots and leathers are given short shrift. Otherwise, it is very thorough, clearly written and well illustrated with 302 black-and-white photographs, some of which are merely pictorial fillers but, for the most part, they are pertinent to the text.

48. KEIG, STANLEY ROBERTSON and text by BOB HOLLIDAY. The Keig Collection: TT Riders and Their Machines 1911 to 1939. 20.5 x 29.5 cm (8 x 11¼") illus pw. Surrey (Great Britain): Bruce Main-Smith & Co., Ltd., 1975.

This "book" consists of an archive of 1800 snapshots of riders and racers on their machines, with pertinent captions as to personal identification, date, race and location on the Isle of Man. Up to 1975, three volumes of this collection have been published.

49. KOCH, DON. Chilton's Complete Guide to Motorcycles and Motorcycling. 17.5 x 26 cm (6-3/4 x 10") dj cloth 197p illus, index. Radnor, PA: Chilton Book Company, 1974.

The author writes for adults who have little or no experience about the purchase, current history, ownership and maintenance, or riding of motorcycles. Only 19 pages are given to competition cycling. A glossary of four pages identifies 69 terms covering motorcycle parts and related references. Sixty black-and-white photographs and graphics illustrate the book but none of the pictures seem more than space fillers. While they are adequate, a photography editor would have enhanced the book by matching illustrations and the well-done text.

50. KOSBAB, WILLIAM H. Motorcycle Dictionary/Terminology. 13.5 x 21.2 cm (5 x 8¼") ppw 363p. Orange, CA: Career Publishing Inc., c. 1986.

While I did not find identifications for a couple of motorcycle brands (Phillips or Reliant), this dictionary of terms, symbols, measures, and names is pretty well exhaustive and seems pertinent to both the general reader and the technician. The book fills a large gap from mechanic to consultant and has been compiled by a highly qualified professional teacher and writer in the motorcycle industry.

51. LACOMBE, CHRISTIAN. The Motorcycle. 21 x 30 cm (8¼ x 11-3/4") dj cloth 237p illus. New York: Grosset & Dunlap, 1974.

A yearly chronological history covers the motorcycle's development from 1896 to 1936, after which descriptions cover individual post-World War II bikes of major manufacturers, with their distinctive engineering differences and weights and their histories. The rest of the book depicts racing and cycling with about a hundred pages of action photographs with introductory texts, and closing with lists of champions from 1962 to 1972 and a brief consideration of the show bike or chopper.

52. LEAVITT, LANE and LEN WEED. Motor Cycle Trials.

Techniques and Training. 21.5 x 27.7 cm (8½ x 11") ppw 161p illus. Tarzana, CA: Motor Cycle Trials, P.O. Box 241, 1978.

The authors promote the chance for riders "to test themselves and improve their skills" in competitions spread out in many areas so that trials will become "a true international sport." To propagate this, the book details, with profuse illustrations in black and white, every kind of difficulty in terrain that the reader can think of and many he would not want to think of.

International champions from 1965 through 1977 are listed in about 337 listings in the final two pages.

53. LOVIN, ROGER. The Complete Motorcycle Nomad. A Guide to Machines, Equipment, People and Places. 14.5 cm x 21.5 cm (5-3/4 x 8½") dj 308p. Boston: Little, Brown and Co., 1974.

The author (who has done a few drawings for the book) covers every aspect of long-distance touring: clothing, shelter, medicine, camping, equipment, troubleshooting, both in cities and between them. Further sources of information are listed in an appendix.

54. LYON, DANNY. The Bikeriders. 16 x 23.5 cm (6¼ x 9¼") ppw 94p; 17 x 24 cm (6-3/4 x 9½") dj cloth 94p. New York: Macmillan, 1968.

The first 50 pages are a portfolio of portraits of members of a motorcycle club whose identity as far leftist "outlaws" seems synonymous with the insecurity of far rightest conservatism. Their simplicity--or boredom --seems only to be shaken or alleviated by the titillation in the prospect of a violent--hence "heroic"--death. Such ideas are not without some possible depth but as a way of life it seems too thin to be the subject for a book.

The remaining pages comprise dismal biographies of the riders whose lives seem to be handicapped by misfortune or by a lack of both opportunity and intellectual perspective, although the author professes that the book is "an attempt to record and glorify the life of the American bikerider." However, the 17 biographies--while illustrating the indomitable human temperament and dedication to an exclusively narrow cause--arouse our commiseration, if not pity or fear, rather than any sense of glory because the cause has become a private and introvertive one instead of an expanding and broadening interest. The accounts do document, perhaps, the spirit of the lonely man and the mystery in the mystique of the motorcyclist as soloist or as a dependent club member. While the overall philosophy of the group in this book seems one of personal license as against public freedom, the reader can easily understand the impulse toward the "justice" of being a self-styled "outlaw" as well as understand his own reservations about ever being the victim of the outlaw's own selfish practice of vindication, revenge, and, finally, injustice, no matter how the outlaw may explain it away, or, as here, have it explained away for him.

55. MACAULEY, TED. Mike the Bike Again. The Story of Mike Hailwood's Return to the TT. 14.5 x 22 cm (5-3/4 x 8-3/4") dj cloth 87p illus. London: Cassell Ltd., 1980.

While the FIM (Fédération Internationale Motocycliste) had removed the Manx Grand Prix status (the race for amateurs) over the TT (Tourist Trophy) course because over a hundred motorcyclists had lost their lives there, Mike Hailwood came out of comparative retirement after eleven years at age 38 to compete on the Isle of Man again. The author describes the preliminary discussions, practice, and the arrangement with sponsors, officials, and news media in the first 45 pages, and then the actual races in 1978 and 1979.

Written by Hailwood's manager and partner, the book gets the reader involved in the pressures and the euphoria of winning, as well as the self-criticism in losing --as he did for the first time in his last race at the TT.

56. _____. The Yamaha Legend. 17.5 x 23.7 cm (7 x 9-3/4") dj cloth 248p. New York: St. Martin's Press, 1979.

Yamaha's musical instrument background is a story in itself: its logo has three criss-crossed tuning forks.

The historical facts and behind-the-scenes excitement of racing and rivalries are thoroughly presented, from the company's first venture into motorcycles to its international triumphs with amazing riders like Itoh, Phil Read and Bill Ivy competing with Mike Hailwood or Jim Redman. Two separate chapters are devoted to Jarno Saarinen, to his fatal crash, and to Giacomo Agostini. Other more recent riders covered are Rodney Gould, Kel Carruthers, Kenny Roberts, Johnny Cecotto and a chapter is given to Don Vesco and his 300-mph speed record.

The book closes with a technical report on the development of two-stroke engines. While published in New York, the text has British spelling and money is given in pounds.

57. MANN, DICK with JOE SCALZO. Motorcycle Ace. The Dick Mann Story. 15 x 21.5 cm (6 x 8½") dj bds 198p illus. Chicago: Henry Regnery Co., 1972.

Dick Mann's biography captures the "mystique" of wanting to race and the vicissitudes in doing so. The personal narrative is lively and the reader gets to know what it's like to pursue the racing life, to be among other men with the same interest, and how to face retirement (you don't).

Of interest is the dedication to the philosophy of competition which consists here not of putting the other fellow down or in having won races, but in the immediate compulsion in simply winning.

There are 16 pages of photographs.

58. MARRIOTT, ANDREW, editor. The Sheene Machine. 14.5 x 22 cm (6 x 8-3/4") dj cloth 138p illus index. London: Pelham Books, 1979.

The first two chapters of this anthology are not about the racer, Barry Sheene, so much as about the techniques of cornering and passing--written by Peter Clifford--and about the technical engineering specifications and experiments with Sheene's Suzuki racing machines--written by Leonard Setright.

A sensible review of Sheene's personality is given in Dr. Colin Brewer's chapter, "Sheene: A Psychologist's View." Alan Minter compares the risks and motivations of his boxing with Sheene's racing, while Kenny Roberts' comments on competing with Sheene are transcribed into a running dialogue by John Brown of <u>Motorcycle Racing</u> magazine. A television interview with Michael Parkinson summarizes Sheene's public career, and an informal study by Berry Ritchie concerns itself with the economics and marketing (toys and cologne) of the Sheene name. Two others--one by Andrianne Blue-- are a kind of literary profile and--by Bob Andrews--a lively account of a winning day at the races.

Andrew Marriott finishes his anthology with a chapter on the racer's mother, one on the dual relationships of riders, Sheene in particular, on both two wheels and four, on Sheene's superstitions, and a closing chapter on his general home-life.

Thirty-five black-and-white photographs are contained in two signatures, and a fine portrait of Sheene in color fills the back side of the dust jacket.

59. MINTON, DAVE. Motorcycles of the World. 23. x 30.5 cm (9 x 12") dj cloth 64p illus. (Great Britain): MacDonald, 1981.

Specifications are listed for 132 motorcycles manufactured in 13 countries and pictured in 52 color and 68 black and white photographs. The countries include India (with the Enfield 350 Commuter Tourer) and Holland (with a moped and a 50cc motocross), as well as Austria, Czechoslovakia, France, East and West Germany, Great Britain, Italy, Japan, Spain, Sweden and the United States.

The author concludes each listing with remarks on unusual features, if any, and a brief but interesting comment on manufacture, performance, design or some incidental history. The book ends with a list of English dealers and prices in pounds.

60. MORLAND, ANDREW. Custom Motorcycles. Street Bikes On Show. 21 x 22.8 cm (8¼ x 9") ppw 128p illus. London: Osprey Publishing Ltd., 1983.

A sumptuously printed book, one can't resist turning the pages. While produced in England and Hong Kong, only four of the 120 color photographs are outside the American scene. Close-ups and full-length portraits of bikes and riders illustrate the American predilection for personalizing and "humanizing" stock bikes with both decorative and meticulously pictorial paint jobs, metal engraving, chrome plating, and accessories. This care and concern seems in a traditional line of folk art; a century ago locomotives were similar objects of attention, if not so lavishly done. In many cases the bikes here become caricatures of themselves, as if they were designed by the cartoonist, Saul Steinberg, or Ronald Searle. The design work is often amusing and occasionally beautiful in its vision of the machine as an object of art, but the craftsmanship is always awesome. This book is a fine documentation of the phenomenon of the elaborate "chopper" which, two or three decades ago, hardly existed except as a mechanical necessity or utilitarian improvement.

61. MORLEY, DON. Crescent Color Guide to Motorcycling. 23.5 x 32.5 cm (9¼ x 12-3/4") dj illus bds 80p illus. New York: Crescent Books, 1982.

Brief histories are deftly given in regard to motorcycling as a sport, mechanical development, vintage nostalgia, leisure interests, and racing in its various forms. Seventeen pages are taken up with major racing circuits with accompanying diagrams of the individual tracks of Monza Autodrome near Milan, Italy, Daytona, Florida, Spa Francorchamps in Belgium, Assen in Holland, Nurburgring, Germany and the Isle of Man. The book closes with eight pages on motorcycle racing personalities. The author is both a professional photographer and writer in the field of motorcycling. Eighty-nine well-selected pictures are in color and 18 old-time photographs are printed in sepia.

62. MOSS, STERLING and MIKE HAILWOOD; JOHN THOMPSON, editor. Racing And All That. 14.5 x 22 cm (5½ x 8-3/4") dj cloth 155p illus. London: Pelham Books, 1980.

As the order of the names implies, this book is mostly about Moss, the car racer. Only ten pages deal with Mike Hailwood, the motorcyclist, who recalls some tight spots in competition and the personalities of past competitors. He writes, "I do not believe the majority of today's lads are sticking their necks out as much as we did.... We used to ride like that [giving it everything] all the time--not just now and then, but regularly. I hate to get morbid about it, but why is it that so few racing motorcyclists are killed these days? ... really it's only luck that has allowed me to survive until now."

In another context Hailwood has expressed fear and caution but perhaps this emphasizes the danger rather than avoiding it. If luck is finally the one ingredient necessary for survival, as Hailwood claims, then the psychological tug toward what Balint calls in his study, Thrills and Regressions, the "sexual thrill" as in Russian roulette is not as sublimated as one would suppose. Most of us tend to conclude that the sport is a youth's game not only in the matter of years but in the sense that it is only the very young who feel they can afford a disregard for violence to the body. The young feel not only basically immune to death but at the same time victorious over it when a deliberate exposure to and escape from it "proves" that immunity. Perhaps, too, the risks that are taken fulfill a need for an ultimate cause which the sophistication of civilization has removed. Having no supreme reference in our societies or social functions in which we can believe, we possibly turn to the one indisputable truth that remains and so occupy ourselves, almost out of boredom as it were, with our deaths by seeing how far we can extend the risk to life without losing the game. The immediacy of this appeal seems, in most cases, to replace an interest in education as such. A common reaction for the racing motorcyclist, according to this observer's reading, is that school is restrictive and binding, as a book itself is pressed, compacted and bound, while racing is a form, as the biographies frequently say, of "freedom" and release, as the machine itself is a purveyor of movement and weightlessness. Along with this comes the feeling of bodily and mechanical control over technique and technology, if not, indeed, the illusion of individual control over a contemporary world of mass-production, anonymity, and soullessness.

Without these attractions, the motorcycle seems merely an unnecessary form of transportation and the racing of them merely another artificial form of competitive games. Whether one likes or dislikes one aspect or another, the rationale seems doomed to always remain as inexplicable for the one side as it is for the other!

Hailwood goes on to say that in regard to the risks of "horrendous consequences," one has to "not just accept them, but indulge in them.... Otherwise there's surely no point."

The book closes with Hailwood's remark that "because the things are so very powerful ... you have to be a very special kind of lunatic [to ride as near to the limit as possible]. And I know for certain that I am profoundly happy it is them and not me out there right now."

An appendix lists 78 of Hailwood's motorcycle racing successes from 1959 to 1979, as well as his racing-car records.

63. MUTCH, RONNIE. The Last of the Great Road Races. The Isle of Man TT. 15 x 21 cm (6 x 8¼") ppw 135p illus. London: Transport Bookman Ltd, 1975.

As a professed outsider, the author's approach is a sometimes disarmingly different one although an "insider" remarks that the author's "technical knowledge seems a little lacking." He persists nonetheless in documenting, through vignettes, the mystique of the 1974 competition on the Isle of Man and touches on a couple of aspects he might have pursued further (but perhaps in another context), such as [white] male chauvinism in a motorcycle veterans' club, the fact that the ferry passengers to the Island "were a leather fetishist's dream" and that the "threat of death was almost a sexual thrill in the air." These vignettes serve as a kaleidoscopic impression of the panoramic blur and the individual focus of the week of preparation and practice as well as of the race itself, giving to the reader a believable feeling for the place and the event.

The text should have been proofread once more, however, to weed out jarring errors.

64. OLIVER, SMITH HEMPSTONE and DONALD H. BERKEBILE. The Smithsonian Collection of Automobiles and Motorcycles. 21 x 23.6 cm (8¼ x 9¼") dj cloth 164p. Washington, D.C.: Smithsonian Institution Press, 1968.

Five early motorcycles are presented in photographs: a crude velocipede of 1869, a 1902 Indian, a Harley-Davidson and Pope of 1913, and a Cleveland from 1918 in about as many pages. The remainder of the book covers antique automobiles and trucks, a couple of motorized tricycles, a bicycle and a scooter.

65. OLNEY, ROSS R. Light Motorcycle Riding. 20.4 x 28 cm (8 x 11") ppw 112p illus. New York: Macmillan, 1967.

Shunning the "behemoth" as having "nearly died of over-power and poor citizenship," the editor favors the 50cc to 305cc lightweight motorcycle and, after a brief history, discusses purchasing, riding, safety, service, and group activities such as clubs and competition.

66. PARKER, TIM. Japanese Motorcycles. 21 x 23 cm (8¼ x 9") ppw 120p illus. London: Osprey Publishing Limited, 1985.

This is primarily a glossy picture book on the heavyweights of four brands: Honda, Kawasaki, Suzuki and Yamaha, but the captions and shots taken in France, England, and California are especially knowledgeable and informative although the last punctuation mark is distractingly omitted. Was this typographical "style"? Also, there should have been one more proofreading.

The book approaches the subject with the inquiring eye of the aficionado who, like most motorcycle enthusiasts, always likes to stop and look at a good-looking machine wherever it may show up. All the 117 pictures are "candid" in that their "portraits" seem to have been arranged by chance, although they have been photographed carefully and, apparently, as carefully selected.

The author gives his frank opinions on performance and styling. This is a happy browser's book.

67. PATRIGNANI, ROBERTO and CARLO PERELLI. Color Treasury of Motorcycle Competition. Off-Road Riding and Racing. 22.5 x 30 cm (8-3/4 x 11-3/4") ppw 64p. New York: Crown Pub., 1974.

Translated from the Italian, only the last four pages relate to the American scene, but description and advice are provided for motocross, trials, speedway, ice, mountain and side-car racing. Seventy-six color photographs supplement black-and-white photographs.

68. _____ and MARIO COLOMBO. Motorcycles. Classics and Thoroughbred. 23 x 30.5 cm (9 x 12") bds 64p illus. New York: Golden Press, 1972.

    The foreword describes the book as "an introduction to the most representative and prestigious models of the world" for "those who have just discovered the motorcycle."
    Lightweight machines are included "because these are the machines of the very young" who have not been able to own the larger ones.
    Although a translation from the Italian, the text is well written and captures the romance of the subject: "There are few vehicles that require as much intelligence, reflex action, and sheer nerve as the motorcycle. Everything is left to the instinctive judgment of the driver who has to decide the exact moment at which to open the throttle, and work the gear change, clutch, and brake to make his driving a real work of art."
    Engineering principles are intelligently communicated in the first 16 pages while the remainder of the book consists of colored photographs with specifications and comments on famous makes.
    This book also was available in the United States with the cover title, Color Treasury of Motorcycles under the Crescent Books imprint.

69. PERRY, ROBIN. The Road Rider. A Guide to On-the-Road Motorcycling. 16 x 23.5 cm (6¼ x 9¼") dj cloth & bds 152p illus. New York: Crown Publishers, 1974.

    Major considerations are covered: purchase, maintenance, accessories, riding safety on the highway, with passengers, in rain, snow, deserts, mountains, and riding at night. One chapter is devoted to learning how to ride. The author is a professional photographer and the book is well illustrated with 93 black and white photographs.

70. _____. The Woods Rider. A Guide to Off-the-Road Motorcycling. 16 x 23.5 cm (6½ x 9½") dj cloth 144(8)p illus. New York: Crown Publishers, 1973.

    This well-illustrated book (78 photographs) begins

with the purchase of an off-the-road bike. Pages 24 to 134 cover beginners' as well as experts' techniques and precautions for all seasons. The book ends with descriptions of kinds of off-the-road competitions. Eight pages in the back are reserved for the reader's notes.

71. PIRSIG, ROBERT M. Zen and the Art of Motorcycle Maintenance. An inquiry into Values. 14.5 x 21.5 cm (5-3/4 x 8½") dj 412p. New York: William Morrow, 1974.

The author draws on the American tradition for inventiveness, practicality, and that kind of modest honesty that makes a United States citizen his own man with neither pretension nor subservience, in either the sciences or the arts. In fact, the book couldn't be more American in the laudatory sense of that sometimes self-conscious category.

The focal point of the narrative is a road trip across country, flashbacks on the rider's life, and reflections provoked by the maintenance of the bike. In his mechanical problems as well as in his intellectual ones, the writer presents the historical conflict between classical thinking (i.e., reality as law, as theory, structure, technology, science--the motorcycle as a kind of mechanical universe) and romantic feeling (i.e., reality as based on purpose, the total experience of a thing, expression, humanistic concerns--the motorcycle as a man's personal possession).

Robert Pirsig takes these two kinds of reality--so often in social conflict with each other--and reconciles the classical harmony of science with the romantic harmony of art through what is their common concern to us, and makes either area equally meaningful to man, himself. This common concern in both science and art, Pirsig says, is the sense of quality--that is, betterness, or selection--choosing one detail out of infinite possibilities to create sensible improvement and knowledgeable judgments. Otherwise, there is no difference, in the matter of truth, or in the matter of discerning any sense of reality, between a pile of nicely milled lumber and a house. In between, the thing requires good carpentry as well as attractive plans. In other words, the use or the application of what we know about science or art is of no value unless we qualify the data we've got on hand, and make them work together. It's a short step from this position to that of zen which, stating it very simply, propounds the adage that anything worth doing is worth doing well. One of Pirsig's analogies, naturally, takes place in a motorcycle repair shop where the radio was blaring, all the tools misplaced, the mechanics talkative and horsing around--and the author's motorcycle all but ruined by the indifferent work on it!

And that's about the gist of the book. What is putting the book into many printings (a special tenth anniversary edition was produced in 1984) is the originality of the thought--reconciling what has been a conflict for most of Western civilization. The book is entertaining as well as provocative because the author exploits several literary levels simultaneously: 1) memory and flashbacks; 2) discussions, or asides, on motorcycle maintenance as stimuli for his reflections; 3) action (the book moves through a motorcycle trip from mid-continent to the ocean, with a side-trip for mountain climbing with his young son); and 4) a generally autobiographical account of his thinking, which involves a previous mental breakdown as well as the analytical breakdown of the traditional ideas and studies we all grew up with.

The book is a clever and entertaining fusion of the total man. The layman may easily find it impressive and enlightening. It almost persuades this reader never to kick his bike in anger ever again! Instead, I will now understand it, and, in effect, let it teach me what I need to know--if only Pirsig would stand behind me with his felicitious language! Perhaps then I would take better care of my bike than I do by contemplating science, art, and quality. At least the author makes me want to do so--and that must be one step, however small, toward enlightened bliss in a technological civilization. And to achieve it through contemplation of a motorcycle is, you've got to admit, a provocative thought in itself. In short, this is what you call a good book.

72. RADLAUER, E. and R.S. Chopper Cycle. 18.3 x 25 cm (10 x 7¼") illus bds 48p illus. New York: Franklin Watts, 1972.

All of the photographs are of motorcycles in color on glossy paper in this picture book, but the "portraits" are almost entirely candid shots within showroom interiors and are merely illustrations rather than professional presentations. The text relegates it to the children's book field and its dramatic approach is similarly condescending, as well as unconvincing in tone.

73. REDMAN, MARTIN. Superbike. Modern high performance motorcycles. 24 x 19.5 cm (9½ x 7½") dj cloth 120p New York: Harper & Row, 1975.

Nineteen pages are given over to portraits of contemporary biggies. The text presents descriptions and technical information on the BMW, the Norton, and Triumph, for Germany and England, five makes for Italy and four for Japan, finishing up with the Harley-Davidson.

The book is lavishly illustrated throughout and is beautifully laid out in an oblong format. Unfortunately, it was printed in England and the color photographs lack the snap the pictures deserve.

74. RENSTROM, RICHARD. Great Motorcycle Legends. 21.5 c 27.8 cm (8½ x 11") ppw 128p illus. Newfoundland, NJ: Haessner Publishing, Inc., 1977.

An earlier edition of this book appeared in 1972 as The Great Motorcycles.

About four pages of text and photographs provide a run-down of 22 brands. These are AJS, Ariel, BMW, BSA, Bultaco, Ducati, Greeves, Honda, Husqvarna, Jawa, Lambretta, Matchless, Montesa, Moto Gilera, Moto Guzzi, Norton, NSU, Ossa, Puch, Royal Enfield, Triumph and Velocette. Curiously, the Yamaha, Kawaski and Harley-Davidson are missing. The descriptions include the historical beginnings of manufacture, mechanical evolution, outstanding records in competition, and an overall account of each bike's popularity for various models as well as the economic vicissitudes of the company itself.

While the book is excellent as far as it goes, the data for the most part go only to 1970, excepting a reference to the 1974 demise of the Triumph, but perhaps the intervening period between then and now is needed to establish what facts will have become legends.

Two-hundred-and-three black-and-white pictures are supplemented by 22 in color, with another on the cover. We wish the typeface, otherwise legible, included a dash, which seems to have been replaced throughout by a confusing hyphen.

75. _____. Motorcycle Milestones. Volume I. 28 x 22 cm (11 x 8-3/4") bds 111p illus. Caldwell, ID: Classics Unlimited, Inc., 1980.

    The 1898 English Ariel three-wheeler opens the list of milestones followed by the 1905 Indian, 1910 BSA, 1913 Thor, 1916 Indian, 1916 Harley-Davidson, 1928 BMW, 1929 Cleveland, 1933 Velocette, 1937 Triumph, 1947 Norton, 1949 Ariel, 1949 Indian, 1952 Vincent, 1955 BSA, 1957 Matchless, 1959 Parilla, 1961 AJS, 1962 and 1963 Honda, and the 1975 Norton.

    Twenty-four technically beautiful color photographs of each bike are given full-page presentations but many are ruined by poorly chosen backgrounds that confuse the foreground detail. An otherwise attractively laid-out book, almost a hundred black-and-white photographs and graphics accompany the well-written historical descriptions and abbreviated list of technical specifications.

    Two dozen extra photographs illustrate the opening eight pages on the motorcycle's "Birth and Development," a succinct summary of motorcycle history.

76. REYNOLDS, FRANK. Freewheelin Frank. Secretary of the Angels. As told to Michael McClure. 14 x 21 cm (5½ x 8¼") dj cloth 160p. New York: Grove Press, 1967.

    The clannishness of togetherness, the need for other people's approval, outweighs the narrow if not false sense of independence and self-reliance with which a group endows itself when it sees itself as an isolationist and insular society, whether that group is religious, communal, official, or motorcycle-oriented. In this sense the Hell's Angels is a symptom rather than an aberration as is usually contended, and this book documents both the symptom and the aberration at their weakest either philosophically or rationally, as the practice of self-assertion is confused with the display of physical and visual effect. For any motorcycle enthusiast, this display tends to be a titillating one but, like violence, however persuasive in the immediate circumstance, the longer view soon reveals a short scan in depth and, in variety, an ever-narrowing scope.

77. RIVOLA, LUIGI. Racing Motorcycles. 13 x 19 cm (5 x 7½") ppw 320p illus index. Chicago: Rand McNally & Co., 1978.

   Translated from the Italian, a brief history of racing is followed by histories of racing motorcycles by country (France, United States, Great Britain, Germany, Italy, Switzerland, Austria, Sweden, Yugoslavia, Netherlands, Belgium, Czechoslovakia, Japan, and Spain "in chronological order for the more important countries in motorcycle production." Two illustrators have supplied 282 pictures, mostly colored. Specifications are provided for 192 of the motorcycles presented. A table of world championship riders and brands from 1949 precede the index that concludes the book.

78. ROTH, BERNHARD A. The Complete Beginner's Guide to Motorcycling. 16 x 24 cm (6½ x 9½") dj cloth 174p. Garden City, NY: Doubleday, 1974.

   Information of a non-technical nature is covered in this book. It is a good survey for the novice who wants more background of a general nature. Photographs sensibly point up the text throughout the book.

79. SAGNIER, THIERRY. Bike! Motorcycles and the People Who Ride Them. 19 x 9.5 cm (7½ x 9½") dj cloth 158p. New York: Harper & Row, 1974.

   The sociological impact of motorcycling as represented between the years of the movie production of The Wild Ones in 1953 and, in 1969, Easy Rider, is discussed in regard to the development of the industry, motorcycle gangs, and racing. If one reads between the lines, the author generally accepts if he does not actually approve of the Hell's Angels as larger-than-life, American-hero, wish-fulfillment types but he seems to want to expunge in their stead the taint of "overt or covert homosexuality" and "leather fetishes," and (quoted from an interview) "oral copulation and sodomy." The author's stance on the conflict between conforming to the law and the exercise of complete freedom of action is ambiguous and weakens the book which otherwise is a judicious panegyric of the motorcycle phenomenon and its enthusiasts.

Advice on theft, the purchase of second-hand bikes (buy a new one instead), and choppers closes the book.

The production is illustrated with 68 black-and-white filler photographs only peripherally pertinent to the text. One graphic illustrates the Wankel engine and one chart organizes chill-factor scales. The dust jacket, done in a purple green and brown Art Deco style by Mark Rubin Design, is unusually appealing, for those who feel a book's visual aspects are, in time, an integral part of its contents.

80. SALINGER, PETER H. Motorcycling and the New Enthusiast. 21.5 x 28.5 cm (8½ x 11¼") bds 95p. New York: Grosset & Dunlap, 1973.

An attractively laid out book, it fills a gap for the complete novice, with explanations of the engineering, tools, maintenance, a listing of motorcycles available, and with general information and advice.

81. SANDERS, SOL. Honda. The Man and His Machines. 21.5 x 28 cm (8½ x 11") dj bds 205p illus. Boston: Little, Brown & Co., 1975.

The distinction of this biography is its insight into Soichiro Honda's business philosophy in a world that boomed, was destroyed, and boomed again. The man's psychology and approach to his calling and his personality are fascinatingly described. The book is memorable and inspiring for any motorcycle enthusiast.

82. SCALZO, JOE. The Motorcycle Book. 22.5 x 28.5 cm (8-3/4 x 11¼") dj bds 210p illus. Englewood Cliffs, NJ: Prentice-Hall, 1974.

After the first six chapters summarizing history, types of motorcycles, care, and riding, the following seven are mostly a descriptive and illustrative coverage of competitive riding from all kinds of racing to stunt riding. The many photographs are mostly in color.

83. SCHILLING, PHIL. The Motorcycle World. 22.5 x 28.5 cm (8-3/4 x 11") dj bds 252p illus. New York: Random House, 1974.

The author writes in his introduction, "This book is an interpretation of past and present. It is an attempt to make sense of the past, to understand why the machinery and the sport grew in certain patterns, and to examine the results of that development."

Numerous photographs document the authoritative and well-researched text. The book has many pictorial perks including eight two-page portraits of bikes, six of which are in color.

84. _____. Motorcycles. 11 x 18 cm (4¼ x 7") ppw 159p illus. index. New York: Bantam Books, 1977.

Profusely illustrated in color, this book provides brief analytical descriptions of well-known models and their identifying features under the subject headings: Roadrunners, Sporting Middleweights, Enduros, Motocross and Cross-Country Racers, and finally Championship Motorcycles, represented by 71 motorcycles.

85. SCHLEICHER, ROBERT. Model Car, Truck and Motorcycle Handbook. 18 x 26 cm (7 x 10¼") ppw 161p illus. Radnor, PA: Chilton Book Company, c. 1978.

There are only seven pages on the simulation of parts of motorcycles for the model maker. Two magazines (International Modeler and Scale Models) are recommended for sources but the main advice is "to write every shop in America and England that advertises a catalog," which leaves the reader nowhere. There is no information of consequence on mass production manufacturers, and none on addresses or history. The book is "for builders, not just collectors," but, again, this refers to cars and trucks--not motorcycles. Otherwise the book is handsomely produced but the title just happens to over-reach itself in this instance.

86. SCHNEIDERS, RON. ISDT '73. The Olympics of Motorcycling. The official pictorial record of the 48th International Six Days Trial, Pittsfield, Mass., USA. 17.5 x 26 cm (6-3/4 x 10¼") boxed bds 155p illus. Radnor, PA: Chilton Book Co., 1973.

In covering one event within a six-week production

deadline, the editors claim a "first" in publishing history with their documentation of the first American ISDT in 60 years of this annual competition which consisted in 1973 of 303 riders from 15 countries. The first 70 pages are a descriptive history of the race and the evolution of its rules.

The contest is covered with a day-by-day account up to the presentation of the World Trophy to the Czechoslovakian Jawa Trophy Team and the Silver Vase to the U.S. Husqvarna Vase Team. An 11-page appendix lists the scorings of individuals and teams. Illustrations throughout are in both color and black and white.

87. SCHULTZ, NEIL. The Complete Guide to Motorcycle Repair & Maintenance. 15 x 23 cm (6 x 9") ppw 215p illus index. New York: Arco Publishing Inc., 1980.

How complete is "Complete"? Throughout this book the shop manual for the particular motorcycle is recommended when the references to overhaul get complicated and specialized. This book covers everything up to that point and is an excellent intermediary between the information in the maintenance pamphlet that comes with a new bike and the professional shop manual for it. Schultz is explicit about what things are and what they do for the novice on through to the expert mechanic, engineer or electrician, although the experts will probably have gotten their knowledge elsewhere. One-hundred-and-eighty photographs and graphics illustrate the text. The photographs are a little grey, but clear and pertinent.

87a. SCOTT, MICHAEL and JOHN CUTTS. The World's Fastest Motorcycles. 23.5 x. 28.5 cm (8-3/4 x 11¼") dj cloth 127p illus. Secaucas, N.J.: Chartwell Books, 1986.

The first sentence claims "This is the golden age of motorcycling" and the book confines itself to those bikes that achieve maximum miles per hour, identifies a "superbike" (a 1960's term) as "a vehicle ... of fine engineering and speed ... that nobody needs but every redblooded motorcyclist wants"--although their innovations become standard equipment in time.

A quick photographic survey reviews early bikes in

its captions from the Brough Superior (1930's) to Honda's CBX 1000 (1978). The ten-page text, here, as through the book, covers engineering, design and performance details.

Fifty-eight more pages consist of good color photographs, specifications, and a technical description of these often exotic bikes. In a generally alphabetical order they are: Bimonta SB4 (1983) and DBI (1985), Caviga 650 Alazzurra (1984), Ducati MHR Mille (1984) and Formula One 750 (1985), Laverda RGS Corsa (1983), Moto Guzzi Le Mans 1000 (1984), BMW K100RS (1983-4), R80GS (1980) and Krauser-BMW MKM 1000 (1982), Moto Martin (1979), Harley-Davidson XLCR 1000 (1976), Harris Magnum II (1983), Hesketh Vampire (1983), Spondon Turbo GSX1100 (1980), Honda VF1000R (the VF1000F is also compared favorably), and NS400 (1985), CBX750 (1984), and Aspencade GL1200 (1983), Kawasaki GPz1000R (1985), Z1300 (1979) and Z750 Turbo, Suzuki RG500 Gamma (1985) and GSX-R750 (1985), Yamaha RD1100 (1984), FZ750 (1985) and V-MAX (1984).

Racing bikes are included in another ten-page coverage, specifically: Honda's ELF 2 (1984), NSR5000 (1984) and RVF750 (1985), Suzuki's RG500 (1975) and Yamaha's YZR500 OW81 (1982).

Engines as such and bikes of the future are discussed in two final chapters. This handsomely produced book closes with an index and lists of world champions from 1949 through 1985 in the 500, 250, 125cc categories and the sidecar.

88. SETRIGHT, L.J.K. The Guinness Book of Motorcycling. Facts and Feats. 18 x 24 cm (7 x 9½") dj cloth 257p index. Enfield, Middlesex (England): Guinness Superlatives Limited, 1979.

Four sections comprise the book. The first, "Technical Achievements," is a 28-page summary of motorcycle history. The second, "Personal Accomplishments," is a 56-page alphabetical listing of record-makers, providing racing biographies of 107 motorcycle competitors with 55 portraits inserted where pertinent. Two, however, Renzo Pasolini and Dave Taylor, have pictures but no biographical entries. "Brand Marks" consists of 62 pages of history on 13 manufacturers with 62 motorcycle photographs, nine in color and several other graphics, concluding with a massive 15-page list of apparently all makes. The last section, "Sport and Play," covers speed records in 66 pages through text and tables in every kind of competition from the sketchy 1920's to the better documentation of the late seventies, including figures on international motorcycle production.

89. _____. Twistgrip. A Motor Cycling Anthology. 16 x 24 cm (6¼ x 9½") dj cloth 150p illus. London: George Allen and Unwin Ltd, 1969.

The short story by the author is, like most such fiction, more a description of riding than it is a literary piece and the vicarious thrill, even so, goes on a little long. The story serves the subject of motorcycling rather than the other way round.

The book is oriented toward the English view, the English vocabulary and a refreshingly unabashed assumption that the average motorcycle enthusiast reading this book would not feel embarrassed at the fairly numerous references and quotations from poetry--Kipling, Gray, Blake, Shakespeare--where American references I have seen elsewhere (to T.S. Eliot, for example) have that condescending, if not snickering, attitude that covers a fear of education, intelligence, and of a civilized depth of experience.

T.E. Lawrence's famous race with an airplane is included here. Twenty various accounts cover careers, anecdotes, racing (including side-cars), record-making, test-riding, and engineering. The biographical essays, "Reminiscences" by John Griffith and "Amende Honorable" by "R.B." in an otherwise easy-going and pleasant book are difficult to read because of the use of English abbreviations and circumstances. (The increasing linguistic similarities or dissimilarities between English and American English is an old debate that could begin anew here in regard to both technical terms and jargon and lingo.)

Four articles grouped under the section, "Machines," give detailed facts on the history of development from the early motorized bicycles.

Two aspects of motorcycling are summed up in the last article by Andrew Duncan: "It is pointless to compare the advantages of motorcycle racing with the risks. For the riders, it is its own justification. For spectators

... it's a blood sport.... People are there to see someone come off.... Then they're happy."
The illustrations (24 with 2 in color) are of some interest but not essential or very pertinent to the book itself.

90. SHEDENHELM, W.R.C. The Motorcycle and Trailbike Handbook. 10.7 x 18 cm (4¼ x 7") ppw 191p illus. New York: Pyramid Pub., 1976.

Various uses and their proper design for that use are defined for varieties of motorcycles. There is a check list for used bike performance and maintenance. Thirty-four brands are described very briefly with minimum specification charts which only serve to familiarize the reader with an overall view of the industry in general. Information on competition kits for changing the engineering of the stock bike oddly precedes chapters on learning to ride, tools, and maintenance. The book is filled out with 16 pages of 54 miscellaneous photographs of models and racers and chapters on races, records, and riders. Two chapters cover off-road riding and camping. A list of the addresses of manufacturers closes the book.

91. SHEENE, BARRY with IAN BEACHAM. Leader of the Pack. 15.5 x 24 cm (6 x 9½") dj 188p illus. London and Sydney: Queen Anne Press, 1983.

The book is nicely handled by the co-author, opening with a dramatic racing accident with its after-effects and analyses, then turning to biography as such. With parental support and his father's experience as a tuner, and unahppy at school, Sheene discovered he was a "natural" and rose, from his start in 1967, to world prominence. Continuous injuries discussed in the book evoked in this reader the affinities that exist between the exposure to serious danger and the exultation of being alive and in control--surely a definition of "the thrill" as well as "the win."
Relationships with his Suzuki sponsor (and Yamaha 1980--1982), and fellow competitors provide a blow-by-blow account of Sheene's career. His physical and psychological preparations before and methods during racing for the rider and the machine are confided to

46 / Motorcycle Books

the reader, as are Sheene's opinions (and those of Kenny Roberts) on safety precautions set up or not set up by the FIM (Federation of International Motorcyclists). An "I-told-you-so" attitude is engaging, rather than defensively irritating--possibly because of the adroit writing by Beacham. The chapter, "Why I Do It" is particularly articulate.

The dust jacket is appalling for anyone who relies on his fingers for any endeavor as the illustration on it shows Sheene looking, bemused, at his mutilated hand, which he holds up for the photographer.

A signature within the book presents 33 snapshots. The only item lacking is a view of Gladys Cooper's extensive house that the author bought, which could have replaced the photograph of the Rolls Royce, in this reader's opinion.

92. SHILTON, NEALE. A Million Miles Ago. 18 x 24 cm (7 x 9½") dj bds 300 p illus index. Sparkford (England): Haynes Publishing Group, 1982.

The author worked for Triumph and BMW in England for 22 years as a sales representative over much of the globe and this provided him with much of the inside experience with riding, and with racing and dealer friends. Some of the references to places and names are a little special for American readers but the subject and enthusiasm are universal. The prototype of the 650 Thunderbird was the author's own bike modified. Very popular in America, as most of us know, the bike's name is derived from that of an Indian chief and proved its claim for 500 miles at over 90 mph at the French track, Montelhery, in September 1949. The author introduced, as well, the first fairing and radio communication for the police market and provided the name, Bonneville, for that later machine, "the most successful of all British motorcycles," in honor of the Utah flats where the Thunderbird made the speed record of 214 mph in 1956. (A Triumph surpassed this in 1962 at 224 mph.)

Misunderstandings and a basic disinterest in motorcycling among new executive personnel after Triumph was sold to BSA as a subsidiary are aired as these seem to have contributed to the continuous disintegration of management decisions and finally the demise of the important part of British motorcycle manufacturing.

Believe it or not, besides more serious prejudices exercised, according to the author, company employees were instructed by the new, non-riding, executives to hide their riding gear and motorcycle outfits lest the factory offices be associated with those kind of people who ride motorcycles!

There are 145 photographs but the reproduction is occasionally poor and the proofreading was sometimes negligent. But the book is entertainingly written by an intelligent man and it is historically interesting in regard to the inside story of the failure of the Triumph company. Seven-page index.

93. SMITH, LE ROI. Fixing Up Motorcycles. 14.5 x 21 cm (5½ x 8¼") dj cloth 202p illus. New York: Dodd Mead, 1974.

The first 34 pages of Chapters 1 and 2 consist of history and purchasing. The 16-page "portfolio" of photographs, while interesting, actually illustrate various uses of different kinds of bikes and portraits of antique bikes--rather than fixing them up.

Following this, basic checks are outlined for fixing up a used bike. Two- and four-stroke engines are described with a summary of engine repair, troubleshooting, and tune-ups. General advice is given for transmissions, sprockets, chains, brakes, tires and wheels. The last five chapters, 9-13, describe the varieties of trail, dirt, mini- and street bikes, choppers and touring bikes, closing with 10 pages of advice on altering (chopping) large bikes.

A second section of photographs attempts to illustrate procedures for maintenance, repairs and modifications with 12 pan-shot pictures out of a total of 35. In short, the book is not a how-to, but merely a discussion of fixing up motorcycles.

94. SPIEGEL, MARSHALL. The Cycle Jumpers. 10.5 x 17.5 cm (4 x 7") ppw 174p illus. New York: Scholastic Book Services, 1973.

The language talks down to the reader in that rosy glow that writers for youngsters seem to feel they need to adopt to make their subjects easily palatable for the immature--be they children, or the adult censors of public libraries. Real issues are therefore often avoided. As an instance, in this book, when Evel Knieval has been imprisoned for stealing, the author glosses this over with the remark that "most of the juvenile delinquency charges against him in those days weren't serious" (page 20). We are not told which ones were serious. For a book ostensibly aimed at young readers, one doesn't mind whatever truth is here, but one does mind the evasion and dissembling of it. Again (page 43), the subject's involvement in a brawl is lauded when his assailants are hospitalized.

Otherwise, the author documents fairly well the compulsion to make competitive records as Knieval and another motorcycle jumper, Gary Wells, do. The first 91 pages cover Knieval. Biographical material on him is sparse and is more thorough on Gary Wells in the rest of the book.

The accounts close with events up to 1973. Fifty-three nice photographs illustrate the text but the reproduction, being on pulp paper, is poor.

95. STEPHENS, PATRICK, LTD. Best of British. 19.5 x 24 cm (8 x 9½") dj cloth 158p illus. Bar Hill, Cambridge (England): Patrick Stephens Ltd., 1980.

An important segment of motorcycle history is encompassed in this survey of 38 motorcycles of about 16 well-known English brands. An interesting account of owners' opinions is included in separate inserts besides general histories, and specification of each bike illustrated.

An account of the gradual decline and subsequent company consolidations of the industry in England is given up to 1978.

The black-and-white portraits throughout the book are unfortunately amateurish and the layout struck this reader as uninspired, if not crude. The bold type, as one opens the book to the half-title page, was infested with dust marks indicating an indifferent and careless printing job. The book is basically a reprint of casual newspaper articles from Motor Cycle News and this seems to have inhibited a more careful presentation in the matter of printing, color, design, and photography. However, this survey fills a gap and provides a thorough background to what is, for the American reader, usually a vague territory of knowledge and history.

96. STREAMO, VINCE. Touching America With Two Wheels.
22.5 x 28.5 cm (8-3/4 x 11¼") dj cloth 145p. New York:
Random House, 1974.

Basic suggestions for clothing, packing and maintenance are covered. Several travel photographs seem irrelevant to the means of transport and the book tends to be a routine account of any similar trip. However, the rest of the book deals with the round trip, coast to coast, and with the aspects and incidents that motorcycle enthusiasts appreciate and enjoy.

97. SUCHER, HARRY V. Harley-Davidson. The Milwaukee Marvel. 18.3 x 25 cm (7¼ x 10") dj bds & cloth 283(1)p. (England): Haynes Publishing Group, 1981.

The text alone is impressive. If the type had been a normal book size (10 or 11 points instead of 8), the size of this already generous book would have been doubled. Ironically, the account of this most American and almost the most famous of manufacturers has apparently had to find a publisher in England for this exhaustive and objective profile of a company and an industry. Pictures are not however well placed in relation to the text and the captions, being of the same type as the text, are often confusing.

98. TAYLOR, RICH. Photography by DOUG MELLOR. Street Bikes. Superbikes. Tourers. Café Racers. A Golden Wheels Book. 22.5 x 23.5 cm (9 x 9¼") illus bds unpaged (48)p illus. New York: Western Publishing Co., 1974.

Fifty-seven portraits and close-ups in color of high-speed motorcycles are crammed into this browser's book. By "street bike" the author means highway machines for long-distance travel on major thoroughfares. He evaluates the performance of 13 brands with descriptions of 39 models. He also concerns himself with styling and aesthetics, a branch of philosophy in which every bike enthusiast is a connoisseur but which remains, interestingly enough, inexplicable as a discipline or rationale. In this regard, the author expresses himself briefly but convincingly.

99. THIFFAULT, MARK. Motorcycle Digest. 21 x 28 cm

(8½ x 11") ppw 320p illus. Chicago: Follett Publishing Co., 1972.

This compendium does not digest the facts as much as it surveys them overall, starting with an essay on riding in general, aimed at the novice. Purchasing, learning to ride, legalities and various kinds of racing and riding, various aspects of mechanics, maintenance, and shop work get individual chapters. Mini-bikes and towing advice are also covered. Thirty-two pages consist of a photographic album with specifications for 19 brands. The book closes with an address list of sources for accessories and a glossary of cycle terms. This is an excellent book for both the beginner and the old hand, and it is surprising that it has not been more visible and more available at various outlets over the years. This reviewer did not see a copy till 1986. Perhaps an up-date is in the works?

There are 583 photographs, almost all of them pertinent to the text and well placed.

100. TRAGATSCH, ERWIN. The Complete Illustrated Encyclopedia of the World's Motorcycles. 23 x 30 cm (9 x 11-3/4") dj cloth 320p illus. New York: Holt, Rinehart and Winston, 1977.

The first 32 pages provide a history of motorcycle manufacture, with attention to World War I, the twenties and World War II, closing with designers. The next 30 pages is a pictorial presentation in color of "classic bikes" from 1912 to 1975. The rest of the book, page 67 to 320, consists of an illustrated and alphabetical history of 2,500 motorcycle manufacturers from 1894 to about 1975. Leading models are tabulated in four time spans from the twenties to the present, and the book closes with a glossary of miscellaneous terms of reference.

101. _____. The Illustrated History of Motorcycles. 23 x 30 cm (9¼ x 11-3/4") dj bds 64p. London: New Burlington Books, 1979.

Sixty black and white illustrations accompany this history which begins with the first two-wheel, engine-powered vehicle of 1885 (the term "motorcycle" not being used until 1894) and traces early experiments up to World War II in the first dozen pages, which include a brief but interesting chapter--a world survey of the industry's erratic economics. The war period comprises about 475 words. There is a quick run-down of the twenties--"the golden age" for the variety, popularity, and production that were evident. Three more pages cover the motorcycles of different nations used in World War II, and two more comprise a chapter entitled "The Great Designers." Thus, the history is finished in 32 pages. However brief, the fund of knowledge and the depth of the subject is perhaps more than suggested, as the recent library that has come into existence of books on motorcycles proves.

The remainder of the 64 pages of this book is a generous portrait gallery in 40 color photographs of two dozen outstanding "classic" bikes from the Henderson of 1912 to more contemporary representatives of the 1970's.

102. _____. The World's Motorcycles 1894-1963. A Record of 70 Years of Motorcycle Production. 15 x 22 cm (5-3/4 x 8-3/4") dj cloth 192p illus. London: Temple Press Books, 1964.

This amazing compilation lists "nearly 2,000 makes of motorcycle produced up to 1963 in nearly 30 different countries" and includes addresses, production period and facts, figures, and remarks.

By way of a stab at illustration, there are four pages of small silhouettes of 36 antiques and four pages of photographs of 12 more recent motorcycles.

103. VENABLES, RALPH. Schoolboy Scrambling and Other Motorcycle Sports. 19 x 25 cm (7½ x 9-3/4") illus bds 92p illus. Andover (England): Oxford Illustrated Press Limited 1975.

Published in England, this book, which is introduced by Lord Montague, has none of the reticence and caution so often expressed by Americans toward riding. The frontispiece is a photograph of a child about 7, still with baby fat on its cheeks, taking instructions from the author. But, in general, this book is aimed at the grammar-school to early-high-school boy. (No girls seem to be included here.) The 144 black and white photographs illustrate twelve chapters on clubs (36 are listed for England), rules, clothing, practice, competition and maintenance, with the parents' approval and cooperation being understood throughout the book.

104. WAKOSKI, DIANE. The Motorcycle Betrayal Poems. 14.5 x 21.5 cm (5½ x 8½") dj bds 160p. New York: Simon and Schuster, 1971.

Four poems by this well-known poet relate to affairs with motorcyclists. The dust jacket shows the author with a Yamaha. It was also printed as a paperback with the admonition on the cover: "This book is dedicated to all those men who betrayed me at one time or another, in hopes they will fall off their motorcycles and break their necks."

105. WALLACH, THERESA. Easy Motorcycle Riding. 14 x 23.3 cm (5½ x 9¼") bds 160p illus index. New York: Sterling Publishing Co., 1970.

The author, perhaps deserving of another book about herself, has written a step-by-step introduction to riding for beginners, using her experience in her own motorcycle shop and instruction school. The text is printed in comparatively large type and is illustrated throughout with line drawings.

106. WHYTE, NORRIE. Motor Cycle Racing Champions. 19 x 25.5 cm (7½ x 10") dj bds 96p illus. New York: Arco Publishing Co., 1975.

Interviews and biographical material are given on:

Giacomo Agostini (Italy)
Kent Andersson
Mick Andrews (Great Britain)
Chris Baybutt
Mick Butler
Johnny Cecotto (Venezuela)
Roger De Coster (Belgium)
Jack Findlay
Mick Grant
Tom Herron
Mac Hobson
Eero Hyvarinen (Finland)
Ivan Mauger (New Zealand)
Pekka Nurmi (Finland)
Keith Parnell
Phil Read

Andy Roberton
Gene Romero
Ted Scott
Barry Sheene (England)
Nick Thompson
Walter Villa (Italy)
John Williams

Sixteen pages of photographs in color complement many black-and-white action photographs and portraits.

107. WILDE, SAM. Barbarians on Wheels. 25 x 34.5 cm (10-3/4 x 13½") dj cloth 160p illus. Secaucus, NJ: Chartwell Books Inc., 1977.

The search for certainty, the sometimes desperate need for us all, is documented here for its shock value but, like most such treatments, tends to confuse, or avoids, the difference between legal and moral integrity so that the one is identified as the other in the popular stereotype. Consequently, ostracization is enforced, and such phenomena as the Hell's Angels are categorized as a cause rather than as a symptom. At the same time the base appeal to the reader's secret desire to indulge in being an outlaw and to act with impunity beyond the reach of conscience or of sensibility is subtly exploited. It is not that this author equates sensibility with a suit and tie, but rather that the thrill of the risk as in racing is a private "need" and responsibility, and defying death to one degree or another--as the fine performance of any action is, be it the professional pianist on stage or a lone motorcyclist. The difference arises when it is a matter of defying society for selfish ends or of inflating one's ego through destructively vindictive motives. The leather, hair and grease has nothing to do with it except as prejudice in the public eye, even though the leather, hair and grease may indeed be used as flagrant symbols of anti-social thinking and non-conformist acts. (Actually, the Hell's Angels group is, within their own society, extremely conformist as well as introverted.) Such groups yearn for that imaginary kind of certainty that, it seems, can deny death--or at least the fear of it. Unfortunately, this kind of in-group certainty also denies its participants any sense of life outside, except in the sense of saying "shit" in church.

Accepting these premises as a <u>raison d'être</u> for the book, it is beautifully presented in an elaborate format. The inherent and underlying desperation of many of its subjects is successfully avoided as being of any kind of philosophical issue much beyond the adage that the abnormal is always fearful--and sometimes titillating--as it seems to be proven here.

108. WILLIAMSON, MITCH. Safe Riding. Staying Alive on Your Motorcycle. The Complete Safety Manual. 14 x 21 cm (5½ x 8¼") ppw 224p index. New York: Everest House Publishers, 1980.

This book is not for the visually minded; there are no pictures aside from the cover. As the title implies, it concentrates on accident prevention--an area that is often glossed over as a kind of "occupational hazard" in other books. There is a discussion of various conditions of particular accidents, of traffic, of the road itself and of the rider. Under "Riding Double" the author says, ingenuously enough, "I would never ride as a passenger on a motorcycle with anyone" (page 101).

While not overlooked, winter conditions, leathers and heavy machines seem to be outside the author's experience. The book is indexed with a cursory glossary of 26 mostly ordinary terms, lists of magazine publications, associations, information sources and charts of state equipment requirements and licensing.

109. WILLOUGHBY, VIC. Classic Motorcycles. 22.5 x 30 cm (8-3/4 x 12") dj cloth 176p illus. New York: The Dial Press, 1975.

Four loving, double-page, full-color "portraits" of motorcycles grace this book and a fifth extends across the dust jacket, with a dozen smaller portraits among several other action shots. In addition, there are innumerable black-and-white documentary photographs throughout the book. The text covers engineering history in detail on 40 different brands. An intriguing combination of fact and romance has been nicely done.

110. _____. Classic Motor Cycles. 22.2 x 30.2 cm (8-3/4 x 12") dj cloth 208p illus. London: Hamlyn Publishing Group. First published 1975. Second edition, 1982.

This is the first motorcycle book we have seen in

the short history of motorcycle book publishing that has been "recycled." Have we come full circle at last in this new bibliographical category?

This writer thought highly of the book when it originally came out. Editorial changes involve six new entries (Unit New Imperial, Moto Morini single, Moto Guzzi vee-eight, Norton Commando, Kawasaki tandem twins, and Suzuki RG500). These are accompanied by three double-page color spreads, and 13 new color illustrations with 34 new black-and-white ones. One color illustration was exchanged for a more interesting shot of a 1951 Vincent Rapide.

The paper stock has been much improved. The dust jacket has been replaced, however, with three color shots of five bikes, two of them hidden by fairings, and hum-drum type, for the much less busy, large portrait of an antique Douglas with attractive "period" type that appeared in the original design of the 1975 edition.

111. _____. Exotic Motorcycles. 23 x 23 cm (9 x 9") dj cloth 190p illus index. London: Osprey Publishing Limited, 1982.

Well-written, the book provides descriptive accounts from the fifties and sixties of not only the performance of particular machines but the excitement of it all as well. The author runs the following bikes through their paces in demonstration or competition: the experimental NSU prone-positioned "flying hammock," the 100-mile 592cc Matchless Sport Twin, a custom-made fibre-glass-shell-enclosed 350cc Royal Enfield Bullet, the 13-foot 1453cc Drag-Waye for "standing" quarter-mile competitions, the Vincent 1000 with the then speed records of 165 mph (and 162 mph with sidecare on Easter 1975)--as well as some 13 other distinctive motorcycles. The author describes engineering details as well as his own experiences in riding or racing each of these machines.

There are 140 black-and-white photographs, all of which do justice to the author's riding experience and journalistic talent.

112. WILSON, JAMES C. Three-Wheeling Through Africa. 17 x 23-3/4 cm (6½ x 9¼") cloth 351p illus. Indianapolis and New York: Bobbs-Merrill Company, 1936.

This is the account of a trip, by a pair of men with two side-cars, from the African gold coast to the Red Sea. A couple of dozen photographs illustrate their progress. Written in a journalistic gee-whiz style, the means of transportation is incidental to the progress report of this travel book.

113. WINELAND, LYNN. Motorcycle Sport Book. 21 x 27.6 cm (8½ x 11") ppw 192p illus. Los Angeles: Petersen Publishing Co., 1966.

Mainly a picture book of models with articles interjected occasionally, the following year's edition of 1967 (by Bob Greene) seems to have exploited the experience the editors acquired on this one.

114. WOOLLETT, MICK. Racing Motor Cycles. 22 x 29 cm (8-3/4 x 11½") dj cloth 96p index. London: Hamlyn, 1973.

A progressive account of racers and races in Europe since World War II is given with an introductory chapter on the twenties and thirties. A few photographs in the last chapter introduce the American scene of the seventies. A list of the world championship series from 1949 through 1972 is provided. The book is amply illustrated with photographs, most in color, supplemented by a few pictorial drawings.

115. WORTHINGTON-WILLIAMS, MICHAEL, MAX ANSELL, MIKE ATHINSON, and RICHARD HOOK, illus. Cycles and Motorcycles. 22 x 29¼ cm (8-3/4 x 11½") illus bds 62p illus. Glasgow and London: Collins, 1976.

This book gives unusually extensive coverage to the motorcycle's predecessor, the bicycle, from the early 19th century, with its gradual transformation, through one extinct species or another to the full-fledged beast of the 1930's. There is also coverage of the motorized bicycle and the motor scooter. The book closes with a summary of international post-war production. All the illustrations, which decorate every page, are drawings in color.

116. WRIGHT, DAVID K. The Harley-Davidson Motor

Company. An Official Eighty-Year History. 20 x 24.5 cm (7¼ x 9-3/4") dj bds 288p illus index. Osceola, WI: Motorbooks International, 1983.

The first chapter, "Beginnings," covers the industrial development of the Harley-Davidson from motorized bicycle to more recent times. The author uses more discretion in reference to labor and investment problems than the more frank books. Even in this book the Company states possible reservations about the author's "interpretation of the fact," although this book is the one that is "officially authorized." The Company's sensitivity to its attitudes and mistakes seem over-blown inasmuch as there can hardly be any large business in this century that hasn't fought tooth and nail against socialistic ideas or union organizations, and few can be said to have maintained high marks simultaneously over any continuous period of time in both the areas of economic success and imaginative humanitarian development. As proof of this one only needs to consider that the motorcycle manufacturers that have failed are legion.

A description of the details of manufacturing and assembly is given in "Construction," with a run-down of each model from 1903 through 1983 in the chapter "Iron" (which begins explicitly enough with an explanation, as though it were needed, of what the word "evolution" means!).

"Uniforms" covers the use of Harley-Davidsons in the invasion of Mexico, the two World Wars, and for domestic sales to the police. "Dealers" traces the motorcycle boom to 1920, its decline (in competition with the automobile) to the end of World War II and its subsequent establishment as part of a more pervasive national interest. In this book dealer and suppliers' conflicts in the past are not mentioned, but how dealers work currently in their business is described in some detail.

In the chapter, "Restoration," information is given on the specific machines illustrated. A descriptive list has been drawn up of 13 museums that include vintage motorcycles as well as 11 sources for old parts. Sixteen color photographs illustrate restorations and display bikes.

The author loses a little of his objectivity in

58 / Motorcycle Books

"Adornments" when his tone is that of a sales pitch, and also in "Scenes," as he seems unnecessarily defensive in being anti-foreign, anti-stock-machine, anti-college, and pro-in-group. One comes away unfortunately with the impression that self-indulgence among motorcyclists is of a piece with the idea of social and business monopolies, and only when this philosophy reaches the Hell's Angels kind of proportions is there embarrassment about it when the philosophy becomes too visible.

Nine national clubs with descriptions of their interests are listed in "Scenes." The coverage in "Racing" begins with a 1920 racing bike and closes at 1982.

Advertising techniques and problems are treated in "Image." One curious statement, not followed through in detail, that the author considers a problem is: "Fortunately, some bikers may dislike the company, but they love the motorcycles." This is followed later by a list to characterize the Harley-Davidson owner, which includes: "One who sees himself as an individualist, but is a conformist who needs a sense of brotherhood and camaraderie." The ambiguity, for this reader, opens a can of worms.

Movies, actors, and public figures associated with motorcycles are briefly discussed in "Celebrities."

The last chapter details the purchase of the company by AMF, the operation difficulties in competing with the mass production techniques of Japan, the repurchase of the company by the Harley-Davidson people, and the installation of graduated tariffs against imports through 1987.

The book closes with a list of the various specifications for models from 1908 through 1983, and production figures from 1903 through 1981, as well as national racing champions from 1946 through 1982. The last five pages comprise an index.

117. WRIGHT, STEPHEN. American Racer 1900-1940. 29 x 32 cm (11½ x 12½") dj cloth 260p illus index. Huntington Beach, CA: Megden Publishing Co., 1979.

The foreword claims that "here for the first time is a comprehensive photographic record covering all major events of the first forty years of American machines in competition." The first 214 pages are a compendium of photographs of United States racers and motorcycles with well-documented captions.

Hill climbing is brought in briefly in 9 pages, mostly photographs and Class C (lights and other excess parts removed) competition is covered with a short paragraph and four photographs on three pages. Sixteen more pictures depict Indians and Harley-Davidsons with their riders in English competition in 18 pages, Australia in 8 and New Zealand in a dozen more. Brief histories by various writers accompany each section.

As a historical reference, this handsome presentation is a rare collection of photographs all generously laid out, but of necessity, of course, only in black and white. The illustrations begin with a photograph of a 1900 motorcycle--what we might now call a moped. The "bicycle look" is predominant to 1930 when Harley-Davidson's low-slung engine and "automobile" tires could go down the street today without looking primitive or unusual.

The text consists of pictorial captions, giving much detail on the history and performance of daring men and fast machines, 100 mph having been reached as early as 1912. The last 30 pages provide a quick survey of American machines and riders overseas.

Part II

COMPREHENSIVE LISTS, BY TOPIC

Biography

(Beart, Francis)
 Clew, Jeff. Francis Beart--A Single Purpose. 207p, 116 illus.

(Collective)
 Carter, Chris and Fred Clarke and Eddie Fitch. Who's Who of Motorcycle Road Racing. 96p, 81 illus.

 Olney, Ross Robert. Modern Motorcycle Superstars. 112p. New York: c. 1980.

(Hailwood, Mike)
 Hailwood, Mike. The Autobiography of Mike Hailwood. c. 1969.

 Hailwood, Mike and Ted Macauley. Hailwood. 152p, 48 photographs. c. 1970.

 Hailwood, Stan. The Hailwood Story: My Son Mike. c. 1968.

 Macauley, Ted. Mike: The Life and Times of Mike Hailwood. 160p, 40 illus.

 Macauley, Ted. Mike the Bike--Again. 87p, 40 illus.

 (Mike Hailwood at the Isle of Man, 1978. See No. 55.)

(Irving, Phil)
 Irving, Phil. Rich Mixture. Riding and writing about motorcycles.

(Markel, Bart)
 Scalzo, Joe. The Bart Markel Story. 125p, 34 illus.

(McQueen, Steve)
 Nolan, William F. Steve McQueen: Star on Wheels. 159p. New York: c. 1972.

(Miller, Sammy)
  Clew, Jeff. Sammy Miller: The Will to Win. 165p, 180 illus. c. 1977.

(Sheene, Barry)
  Sheene, Barry. Barry Sheene: The Story So Far.... hardbound, 160p, 83 illus, 13 in color. c. 1977.

  Sheene, Barry with Ian Beacham. Leader of the Pack. 188p, 33 photographs. See No. 91.

  Scott, Michael. Barry Sheene: A Will to Win. 223p, 24 photographs.

(Shilton, Neale)
  Shilton, Neale. A Million Miles Ago. 300 p, 140 illus. Involvement with the Triumph, Norton and BMW in Great Britain. See No. 92.

(Surtees, John)
  Surtees, John. John Surtees Motorcycling Book. c. 1970.

(Vincent, Philip)
  Vincent, Philip. P.C.V. Vincent: The Autobiography of Philip Vincent. 167p, 35 photographs. c. 1977.

(Weslake, Harry)
  Clew, Jeff. Lucky All My Life: The Biography of Harry Weslake. 175p, 104 illus. Involvement with the development of the Triumph twin motorcycle engine.

Children

Alth, Max. Motorcycles and Motorcycling. 18.5 x 22 cm (7¼ x 9") bds 90p, illus index. New York, London, Toronto: Franklin Watts, 1979. See No. 2.

Educational Reading Service. My Super Book of Motorcycles and Motorbikes. 19 x 26 cm (7½ x 10¼") ppw 43p illus. Mahwah, NJ: Educational Reading Service, 1971.

Gansberger, Christine. The Motorcycle Coloring Book. 28 x 21.5 cm (11 x 8½") ppw unpaged (24)p illus. Los Angeles: Price/Stern/Sloan Publishers, Inc., 1974. See No. 34.

Schleicherm, Robert. Model Car, Truck and Motorcycle Handbook. 18¼ x 26 cm (7¼ x 10¼") ppw 161p, 128 illus. Radnor, PA: Chilton Book Company, 1978. See No. 85.

Spiegel, Marshall. The Cycle Jumpers. 10.5 x 17.5 cm (4 x 7") ppw 174 p illus. New York: Scholastic Book Services, 1973. See No. 94.

Yolen, Jane. Hobo Toad and the Motorcycle Gang. 62p, illus, Emily McCully. New York and Cleveland: World Pub. Co., 1970.

General Literature

For seasonal information on motorcycle models, road tests, accessories, parts, and news, several nationally distributed magazines are available at every well-stocked magazine stand. Scarecrow Press has put out a thorough bibliography of back issues of such magazines, Motorcycles in Magazines 1895-1983, by Richard D. Christensen.

For specific sales literature on new productions, motorcycle dealers usually have bins of colorful brochures describing the appeal as well as the basic specifications of their own current stock of machines.

The publishers of motorcycle books are indicated in each review provided in this book. For the writer or photographer, specific addresses and the names of editors are available in The Literary Marketplace (R.R. Bowker Company), a standard reference in any public library.

For the purchaser, the outlets listed below are recommended. There is no direct access to every book on the subject of motorcycles and even the alert collector over the last couple of decades must, in all probability, nurse the pain of dozens of omissions on his shelves. The large metropolitan libraries still must aim, it seems, only at a representative--rather than an authoritative--coverage of this recently explosive phenomenon in automative and social history. Perhaps it would take the extra resources of a Malcolm Forbes to do so. If this bibliography has any primary function, beyond the romance of it all, it would be to point a finger in this direction, advisedly as well as accusatively! Certainly, somewhere in this country a library should exist that maintains a definitive concern in this provocative area of literature, technology, and sport.

Bruce Main-Smith Ltd. 312 High Street, Dorking, Surrey, England. The bookshop is devoted exclusively to motorcycle literature and has a global mail-order operation.

Chilton Book Company. Kerry Freeman, Executive Editor. Chilton Way, Radnor, PA 19089; telephone: (215) 964-4000. Motorcycle maintenance manuals and illustrated trade (general public) titles.

Clymer Publications. Box 4520, 12860 Muscatine Street, Arleta, CA 91333; telephone: (818) 767-7660. Repair manuals.

64 / Motorcycle Books

Gordon Book Store. 12 East 55th Street, New York, NY 10022; telephone: (212) 759-7443. Books and magazines.

Roy Harper and Company. 35 Gunter Grove, Chelsea, London SW10, England; telephone: (01) 352-4744. Handles Haynes Super Profile series on vintage motorcycles, as well as other technically oriented books.

S.R. Keig Ltd. Circular Road, Douglas, Isle of Man. Sells direct to motorcyclists and the public prints of their copyright photographs.

Motorbooks International Publishers and Wholesalers Inc. Box 2, Prospect Avenue, Osceola, WI 54020; telephone: (715) 294-3345. Motorcycles histories, manuals and illustrated trade titles.

Osprey Motorcycle Books. 27a Floral Street, London WC2E 9DP, England. Specializes in historical coverage as well as contemporary models. The United States representative is Motorsport. RR 1, Box 200D, Jonesburg, MO 63351; telephone: (314) 488-3113.

History

Allen, C.E. Vintage Road Test Journal. Volume 1, 1904-1930, 165 illus. 70p. Also published: Volume 2, 1903-1930, 200 illus. Volume 3, 1910-1932, 200 illus. Volume 4, 1902-1928, 200 illus. Published circa 1977.

Alth, Max. All About Motorcycles. 209p. New York: c. 1975. See No. 1.

_____. Motorcycles and Motorcycling. 90p. New York: c. 1979. See No. 2.

Arctander, Erik H. The Book of Motorcycles, Trail Bikes and Scooters. 96p. New York: c. 1965.

_____. The New Book of Motorcycles. 112p. New York: c. 1968. See No. 3.

Ayton, Cyril. The Great Japanese Motorcycles. 188p, 200 photographs, 48 in color. Covers Honda, Suzuki, Yamaha and Kawasaki. Bikes and competition through 1980-1981. See No. 5.

_____. Guide to Italian Motorcycles. hardbound 160p, 180 illus. c. 1986. All makes of Italian bikes since 1945.

_____. Guide to Pre-War British Motor Cycles. hardbound 160p, 180 illus. c. 1986.

_____. Japanese Motor Cycles. 164p, 186 illus.

_____. Manx Norton Super Profile. hardbound 8½ x 11" 56p, 93 illus. Opinions, tests, and specifications.

_____. Postwar British Motor Cycles. 164p, 197 illus. 1982.

_____. World Motorcycles, Volume 1. 8½ x 11" approx 260p, 500 photographs. Five hundred current models from 55 manufacturers, with model description.

Bacon, Roy. AJS and Matchless: The Postwar Models. hardbound 7½ x 8½" 150 illus. Osprey Collector's Library.

_____. Ariel: The Postwar Models. hardbound 7½ x 8½" 192p, 150 illus. Osprey Collector's Library.

_____. BSA Gold Star and Other Singles. hardbound 7½ x 8½" 192p, 150 illus. Osprey Collector's Library.

_____. Norton Singles. hardbound 7½ x 8½" 192p, 150 illus. Osprey Collector's Library, c. 1981.

_____. The Norton Twins. hardbound 7½ x 8½" 191p, 150 illus. Osprey Collector's Library.

_____. Royal Enfield: The Postwar Models. hardbound 7½ x 8½" 160p, 150 illus. Osprey Collector's Library.

_____. Suzuki Two-Strokes. hardbound 7½ x 8½" 150 illus. Osprey Collector's Library.

_____. Triumph Singles. hardbound 7½ x 8½" 150 illus. Osprey Collector's Library.

_____. Triumph Twins and Triples. hardbound 7½ x 8½" 192p, 150 illus. Osprey Collector's Library.

_____. Villiers Singles and Twins. hardbound 7½ x 8½" 192p, 150 illus. Osprey Collector's Library.

Battersby, Ray. Team Suzuki. hardbound 7½ x 10" 240p, 250 illus. Covers years of 1952 to 1982 in regard to development of machines and racing teams.

Bayley, Joseph. The Vintage Years at Brooklands. 130 Vintage Racing Motorcycles 1920-30. Illus. c. 1969.

Bishop, George. The Encyclopedia of Motorcycling. 192p. New York: c. 1980. See No. 6.

Caddell, Laurie and Mike Winfield. The Book of Superbikes. 160p, 159 color illus. See No. 10.

Caddell, Laurie. Powerbikes. 160p, 142 illus, 35 in color. Poole: 1981. See No. 12.

Carrick, Peter, compiler. Encyclopedia of Motor-cycle Sport. New York: St. Martin's Press, 1977. As the hyphen in the title suggests, this is a British production but its coverage of all the aspects of racing (races, racers, factories, history and statistics) is world-wide. Includes 39 photographs of individual competitors. See No. 14.

_____. The Story of MV Augusta Motor Cycles. 128p. Cambridge, England, c. 1979.

_____. Superbikes: Road-Burners to Record-Breakers. 80p, 79 color illus. See No. 16.

Carter, Ernest Frank. Cycles and Motor Cycles. 144p. London, New York: c. 1962.

Cathcart, Alan. Classic Motorcycle Racer Tests. hardbound 7½ x 8½" 150 illus. Osprey Collector's Library.

_____. Ducati Motorcycles. hardbound 7½ x 9½" 224p, 200 illus, 8p color. 1983.

Caunter, C.F. Motor Cycles: A Technical History. 165p, 124 illus. 1982 (third edition).

Clymer, Floyd. A Treasury of Motorcycles of the World. hardbound, 240p, 500 photographs, charts and drawings. New York: McGraw-Hill, 1965. See No. 23.

Coombs, Charles Ira. Motorcycling. 96p. New York: c. 1968.

Connolly, Harold. Pioneer Motorcycles. 54p, 50 illus. Fifty motorcycles: drawings and descriptions.

Croucher, Robert M. The Observer's Book of Motorcycles. 192p, 250 illus. Fifty bikes from 15 countries.

_____. The Story of BMW Motorcycles. 7½ x 10" 128p, 125 illus. c. 1980.

Crowley, T.E. Discovering Old Motorcycles. 55p, 37 illus. Vintage motorcycling from United Kingdom.

Currie, Bob. Classic British Motor Cycles: The Final Years. 112p, 138 illus. Twenty-five motorcycles from the National Motorcycle

Museum of Britain. Includes AJS, Ariel, BSA, BMW, Douglas, Frances-Barrett, Excelsior, Greeves, Matchless, Norton, Panther, Royal Enfield, Sunbeam, Triumph, Velocette and Vincent for the '50s and '60s.

_____. Great British Motorcycles of the Fifties. 140p, 176 illus, 19 double-page color photographs. Chapters on Vincent, Sunbeam, Douglas, BSA, Royal Enfield, Ariel, Excelsior, Triumph, Velocette, Norton, AJS and Greeves.

_____. Great British Motor Cycles of the Sixties. 144p, 197 illus, 20 in color. Twenty machines from Matchless, Royal Enfield, Norton, BSA, Triumph and others.

_____. Motor Cycling in the 1930s. 144p, 171 illus. Includes Ariel Square, BSA Gold Star, Levis Model D, Triumph Speed Twin, and Velocette MSS.

Davies, Ivor. Triumph Thunderbird: Super Profile. 8½ x 11" 56p, 90 photographs, 20 in color. "The first of the British superbikes."

_____. Triumph Trident: Super Profile. 8½ x 11" 56p, 90 photographs, 20 in color. "The last of the British superbikes."

David, Pedr. All About Motor Cycles. 76p. Sydney: c. 1974. See No. 27.

Dumble, David B. Classic Motorcycles in Australia. 48p, 93 illus.

_____. Veteran Motorcycles in Australia. 48p, 84 illus.

Engel, Lyle Kenyon. The Complete Motorcycle Book. 195p. New York: c. 1974. See No. 31.

The First Military Machine Series. 64p, 109 illus. Twenty-five military models from 11 makers. Photographs and descriptions of each.

The First Post-Vintage Scene. softbound, 64p, 114 illus. c. 1977. Mostly 1931-1939 machines.

The First Vintage Scene. softbound, 64p, 110 illus. c. 1977. Mostly 1915-1930 machines.

Forsdyke, Graham. Motorcycles. 96p. Secaucus, NJ: c. 1977.

Foster, Gerald. Harley-Davidson: The Cult Lives On. softbound 8½ x 9" 128p, 120 color illus. c. 1985. Sequel to <u>Cult of the Harley-Davidson</u>. See No. 33.

Griffin, Al. Motorcycles. 271p. Chicago: c. 1972.

Griffith, John. Built for Speed (1950-62). 88p, 80 illus. c. 1962. Twenty-four motorcycles.

_____. Famous Racing Motorcycles (1907-61). 108p, 80 illus. c. 1968.

Hailwood, Mike and Peter Carrick. Bikes: Thirty Years and More of the Motor Cycle World Championships. 149p, 21 photographs. c. 1981. Grand Prix racing 1949-1980.

Harper, Roy. Vincent Vee Twins. hardbound 7½ x 8½" 190p, 150 illus. Osprey Collector's Library.

Hartley, Peter. Brooklands Bikes in the Twenties. 244p, 61 illus.

Historical Scrapbook of Foreign Motorcycles. Los Angeles: Clymer Publications.

Hoare, Ron. Speedway Panorama. 167p, 159 illus.

Hodgdon, T.A. The Golden Age of the Fours. softbound 160p, 154 illus. c. 1977. Four-cylinder motorcycles.

Holliday, Bob and S.R. Keig. The Keig Collection. 104p, 200 photographs. vol. 1-3. c. 1977. TT riders and their machines, 1911 to 1939. See No. 48.

_____. Motorcycle Panorama: A Pictorial Review of Design and Development. 112p, 120 illus. c. 1977. See No. 44.

Hopwood, Bert. Whatever Happened to the British Motorcycle Industry? 315p, 208 illus.

Hough, Richard and L.J.K. Setright. A History of the World's Motorcycles (1885-1965). hardbound, 208p, 180 illus. England: Allen & Unwin, 1969. See No. 45.

_____. A History of the World's Motorcycles. 192p, 168 plates, 13 in color, 6 line drawings. New York: c. 1966. See No. 45.

Howard, Dennis. Kaleidoscope of Motor Cycling. hardbound 8½ x 12" 96p, 188 illus. 1910 to the 1950's.

_____. Kaleidoscope of Motorcycling. 95p, 183 photographs. Motorcycling up to the mid 1950's.

_____. Vintage Motor Cycle Album. 96p, 114 illus. Early British exploits. See No. 46.

Howdle, Peter. Best of British: Classic Bikes of Yesteryear. 158p, 120 photographs. Thirty-nine bikes, mostly from '50s and '60s, Great Britain.

Jennings, Gordon. Motorcycles. 164p. Englewood Cliffs, NJ: c. 1981.

Lacombe, Christian. The Motorcycle. 231p. New York: c. 1974. See No. 51.

Louis, Harry and Bob Currie. The Classic Motorcycles. hardbound, 128p illus. New York: c. 1976.

Macauley, Ted. Yamaha. 6-3/4 x 9-3/4" 283p, 170 illus. c. 1984. An up-date of the 1979 book, Yamaha Legend, through 1983. Covers racing, teams, and riders. By Mike Hailwood's manager. See No. 56.

Mackellar, Colin. Yamaha Two-Stroke Twins. hardbound $7\frac{1}{2}$ x $8\frac{1}{2}$" 192p 160 illus. Osprey Collector's Library, 1985.

Main-Smith, Bruce. The First Post-Vintage Racing Scene (1931-1951). 65p, 115 illus. c. 1977.

_____. Roadtests Republished. Volume I (1930-1940). 80p, 150 illus. Eighteen tests. From Motor Cycle Magazine (England).

_____. Roadtests Republished. Volume III (1960-1966). 80p, 175 illus. Eighteen tests. From Motor Cycle Magazine (England).

Military Motorcycles of World War II. 192p, 160 illus. Covers USA, Europe, Russia and Japan, 1939 to 1945.

Minton, Dave. Superbikes. 127p. London, New York: c. 1975.

Morland, Andrew. Custom Motorcycles. $8\frac{1}{2}$ x 9" 128p, 120 color illus. Osprey Publishing, Ltd., c. 1983. Show and street bikes. See No. 60.

Morley, Don. Classic British Trials Bikes. 192p, 165 illus. Osprey Collector's Library. Pre-1965 four-stroke trials bikes.

_____. Classic British Trials Bikes. hardbound $7\frac{1}{2}$ x $8\frac{1}{2}$" 150 illus. Osprey Collector's Library.

Nicks, Mike. Golden Oldies: Classic Bike Roadtests. 160p, 155 illus. Covers 19 machines, including Aemacchi, AJS, Ambassador, Ariel, BSA, Douglas, Matchless, Norton, OK, Royal Enfield, Rudge, Sunbeam, Triumph, Velocette and Vincent.

Norton Motorcycles Pictorial History. hardbound 10 x $7\frac{1}{2}$" 96p, 160 illus. c. 1985.

1951 Catalog of British Motorcycles

Nutting, John. Superbikes of the Seventies. 128p, 125 illus, 21 in color. Northbrook, IL: c. 1978. BMW, Ducati, Harley-Davidson, Honda, Kawasaki, Laverda, Moto Guzzi, MV Augusta, Norton, Suzuki, Triumph, Yamaha.

Page, Victor W. Early Motorcycles: Construction, Operation, Service. softbound, 512p, 300 illus. c. 1977. Reproduced from a 1916 edition.

Parker, Tim. Italian Motorcycles. softbound 8½ x 9" 128p, 120 color illus. Covers modern sports bikes from Benelli, Bimota, Cagiva, Ducati, Guzzi, Laverda, Motini and MV Augusta.

_____. Japanese Motorcycles. softbound 8½ x 9" 128p, 120 color illus. 1985. See No. 66.

Partridge, Michael. Motorcycle Pioneers: The Men, the Machines, the Events, 1860-1930. 112p, 67 illus. c. 1977.

Patrignani, R. and C. Perelli. Color Treasury of Motorcycle Competition. 64p, 130 illus, 79 in color. See No. 67.

Petersen's Three Wheeler. 96p, 235 illus.

Rae, Peter. Honda Gold Wing. softbound 7-3/4 x 10½" 128p, 100 illus, 12 in color. The first book on an individual model of a Japanese motorcycle.

Redman, Martin. Superbike. 120p. New York: c. 1975. See No. 73.

Renstrom, Richard. Great Motorcycle Legends. softbound 128p, 225 illus, 22 in color. c. 1977. Covers 22 machines. See No. 74.

_____. Motorcycle Milestones Vol. 1. softbound and hardbound 111p, 146 illus with 24 full-page color illus. Twenty-four models, 1898 to 1975. See No. 75.

Roberts, Derek. The Invention of Bicycles and Motorcycles. 48p. London: c. 1975.

Sagnier, Thierry. Bike! 158p. New York: c. 1974. See No. 79.

Sanderson, Graham. Superbike Road Tests. 128p, 141 illus, 20 in color. Tests from Motorcycle Weekly: Benelli 900 Sei; BMW R100RS; Ducati Pantah; Hailwood Replica; Harley-Davidson XLS Roadster and FLT80; Honda CB900F-A, CBX1000, CB1100R, and GL1100 Gold Wing; Kawasaki Z1000ST and Z1300; Laverda Montjuic and Mirage TS; Moto Guzzi Spada; Suzuki GT1000ET and GSX1100; Yamaha XV750SE, XS850; and Martini 1.

Scalzo, Joe. The Motorcycle Book. 210p. Englewood Cliffs, NJ: c. 1974. See No. 82.

Schilling, Phil. The Motorcycle World. 252p. New York: c. 1974. See No. 73 and 74.

Schleicher, Robert H. Model Car, Truck and Motorcycle Handbook. 161p. Radnor, PA: c. 1978. See No. 85.

The Second Post-Vintage Scene (1931-1953). 64p, 122 illus. Fifty-two models from 26 makers.

Setright, L.J.K. The Guinness Book of Motorcycling. 257p. Enfield, England: c. 1979. See No. 88.

_____. Motorcycles. hardbound 159p, 140 illus. London: c. 1976. Twenty-four machines before 1978.

_____. Motorcycling Facts and Feats. 257p, 194 illus, 35 in color. Guinness Superlatives Book.

_____. Twistgrip. A Motorcycling Anthology. 1969. See No. 89.

Tragatsch, Erwin. The World's Motorcycles 1894-1963. c. 1968.

_____. The Complete Illustrated Encyclopedia of the World's Motorcycles. hardbound 320p, illus. New York: c. 1977. See No. 100 and 101.

_____. The Illustrated Encyclopedia of Motorcycles. 320p, 900 illus. World manufacturers.

_____. Motorcycles, An Illustrated History. 63p. New York: c. 1980.

Triumph Motorcycles Pictorial History. hardbound 10 x 7½" 96p, 160 photographs. c. 1985.

Vanderveen, Bart H. Motorcycles and Scooters from 1945. 64p, 240 illus. 1976.

_____. Motorcycles to 1945. 64p, 198 illus. c. 1977.

The Veteran Scene. softbound 64p, 126 illus. c. 1977. Pre-1915 motorcycles.

Walford, Eric W. British Motorcycle Industry 1884-1931. Los Angeles: Clymer, c. 1969.

Walker, M. Ducati Singles. hardbound 7½ x 8½" 150 illus. Osprey Collector's Library, 1985.

Walker, Mick. Ducati Twins. hardbound 7¼ x 8½" 192p, 160 illus. Osprey Collector's Library, c. 1985. Covers all bevel and belt drive V-twins and parallel twins from 1970 to 1985. Includes 750, 860, 900, 1000 and Pantah 350, 500, 650 and 750 versions. Racing and development.

Ward, Ian and Laurie Caddell. Great British Bikes. 192p, 320 illus. 1979. Includes AJS, Ariel, Brough, BSA, Douglas, Excelsior, Francis-Barnett, Greeves, HRD, James, Matchless, Norton, OK-Supreme, P&M, Rex, Royal Enfield, Rudge, Scott, Sunbeam, Triumph, Velocette and Vincent.

Willoughby, Vic. Classic Motorcycles, second edition. 8½ x 12" 208p, 290 illus, 35 in color. New York: c. 1975. Examines 46 machines over a 60-year period. Originally published 1975. See No. 109 and 110.

_____. Exotic Motorcycles. 190p, 146 illus. Twenty-four bikes. See No. 111.

Wilson, Steve. British Motorcycles Since 1950, Vol. 1. 128p, 142 illus. Covers AJM, Ambassador, AJS and Matchless (AMC), and Ariel, roadsters of 250cc and over.

_____. British Motor Cycles since 1960, Vol. 2. 216p, 235 illus. Covers BSA, Cotton, Douglas, BMW, Dot, EMC, Excelsior and Francis-Barnett roadsters of 250cc and over.

Woollett, Mick. Superbikes. 64p, 73 illus, 31 in color.

_____. World Championship Motorcycle Racing. 128p, 161 illus, 109 in color.

World Motorcycle Guide. 64p. New York: c. 1977.

Wright, David. The Harley-Davidson Motor Company. hardbound 7½ x 9½" 280p, 250 illus, 14 in color. 1983. See No. 117.

Manufacturers

The prolific production of motorcycles globally has inhibited any overall directory in the standard industry research references. In 1975 The Olyslager Organisation provided an illustrated documentary, "Motorcycles and Scooters from 1945," giving specifics and manufacturing history in very brief form. Two-hundred and fifty models in a 64-page book are accounted for, but the editors call this "only the tip of the iceberg." We are indebted to this book and to L.K. Engel and D. Houlgate's "The Complete Motorcycle Book" (1974) for the list of motorcycle manufacturers below. More local information or the manufacturers themselves appear to be confined to the individual country of origin.

Aermacchi Harley-Davidson
   Varese, Italy.

AJS
   Matchless Motor Cycles Ltd., Plumstead Road, London SE 18, England.

   Triumph Norton, Inc., 2745 East Huntingdon Drive, Duarte, CA 91010; telephone: (213) 531-7138.

   Berliner Motor Corporation, Railroad Street and Plant Road, Hasbrouck Heights, NJ 07604.

Ambassador
   Pontiac Works, Ascot, Berkshire, England.

Apache
   Apache, Ltd., 110 East Santa Anita Avenue, Burbank, CA 91502; telephone: (213) 843-4633.

Ariel
   Great Britain; flourished 1898 (2.25-hp tricycle) to 1965.

Attex
   ATV Manufacturing Co., 1215 William Flynn Highway, Route 8, Glenshaw, PA 15116; telephone: (412) 782-5523.

Benelli
   Pesaro, Italy.

   Cosmopolitan Motors, Inc., Jacksonville and Meadowbrook Roads, Hatboro, PA 19040; telephone: (215) 672-9100.

Bianchi
   Edoardo Bianchi Motomeccania, SpA, Milan, Italy.

Bird
   Bird Engineering, P.O. Box J, Freemont, NE 68025; telephone: (402) 721-8250.

BMW
   Bayerische Motoren Werke A.G., Munich, Germany.

   BMW Plaza, Montvale, NJ 07645.

74 / Motorcycle Books

605 Fifth Avenue, at 50 and 52st Street, New York, NY 10022.

Butler and Smith, Inc., Walnut Street and Hudson Avenue, Norwood, NJ 07648; telephone: (201) 767-1223.

Butler and Smith, Inc., 135 East Stanley Street, Compton, CA 90220; telephone: (213) 638-8508.

Bridgestone
Rockford Motors, Inc., 1911 Harrison Avenue, Rockford, IL 61108; telephone: (815) 298-1220.

Bronco
Engine Specialties, Inc., P.O. Box 260, Cornwell Heights, PA 19020; telephone: (215) 785-3232 or 639-6500.

BSA (Birmingham Small Arms)
Great Britain; flourished 1906 to 1973; Norton-Villiers merged with BSA and Triumph, but dropped both names.

Bultaco
Bultaco International, 5447 Greenwich Road, Virginia Beach, VA 23462; telephone: (801) 499-8501.

Bultaco American West, 2765 Scott Boulevard, Santa Clara, CA 95052; telephone: (408) 241-4672.

Cagiva
Cagiva of North America, Inc., 20030 South Normandie Avenue, Torrence, CA 90502.

Can-Am
Bombardier, Ltd., Valcourt, P.Q., Canada, telephone: (514) 232-2211.

Capriola
Cosmopolitan Motors, Inc., Jacksonville and Meadowbrook Roads, Hatboro, PA 19040; telephone: (215) 672-9100.

Carabela
Carabela East, 131 South Detroit, Bellefontaine, OH 43311; telephone: (513) 593-8226.

Carabela West, 16756 Foothill Boulevard, Fontana, CA 92335; telephone: (714) 822-1056.

Cat
HPE Muskin Corp., 225 Acacia Street, Colton, CA 92324; telephone: (714) 825-8220.

Chaparral
  Chaparral Motorcycle Corp., 5995 North Washington Street, Denver, CO 80216; telephone: (303) 292-1240.

Cheney
  Eric Cheney Developments Ltd.

Cooper
  Cooper Motors, 110 East Santa Anita Avenue, Burbank, CA 91502; telephone: (213) 843-4633.

Cotton Continental
  E. Cotton (Motor Cycles) ltd., Gloucester, England.

CZ
  Czechoslovakia.

  American Jawa, Ltd., 185 Express Street, Plainview, NY 11803; telephone: (516) 938-3210.

  American Jawa, Ltd., 18408 Laurel Park Road, Compton, CA 90224; telephone: (213) 537-8400.

  Union Sales Distributing Co., 630 North Witchduck Road, Virginia Beach, VA 23462; telephone: (804) 499-8961.

Dalesman
  Jeckel Industries, Inc., 38 Everts Avenue, Glen Falls, NY 12801; telephone: (518) 793-5181.

DKW
  Hercules Distributing Co., 9827 Mason Avenue, Chatsworth, CA 91311; telephone: (213) 882-8272.

DOT
  Great Britain; flourished circa 1920's.

Ducati
  Ducati Meccanica SpA, Bologna, Italy.

  Berliner Motor Corp., Railroad Street and Plant Road, Hasbrouck Heights, NJ 07604; telephone: (201) 288-9696.

Dune Cycle
  Allied Mechanical Products, Division of Tower Industries, 13623 Pumice Street, Santa Fe Springs, CA 90670; telephone: (213) 921-6675.

DWK
  Auto Union, Ingolstadt, Germany.

Eso
> American Jawa, Ltd., 185 Express Street, Plainview, NY 11803; telephone: (516) 938-3210.
>
> American Jawa, Ltd., 18408 Laurel Park Road, Compton, CA 90224; telephone: (213) 537-8400.
>
> Union Sales Distributing Co., 630 North Witchduck Road, Virginia Beach, VA 23462; telephone: (804) 499-8961.

Excelsior
> Excelsior Motor Co., Tyseley, Birmingham, England.

Fantic
> Fantic Motor SpA, Fabbrica Veicoli Ricreativi, Barzago, Como, Italy.

FN
> Fabrique Nationale d'Armes de Guerre SA, Herstal, Belgium.

Francis-Barnett
> Great Britain; flourished circa 1920's.

Gemini
> San Tong Co., 15514 South Figueroa Street, Gardena, CA 90247; telephone: (213) 532-1780.

Gilera
> Italy

Gillet
> Herstal, Belgium.

Greeves
> Motor Cycles of Thundersley (later Benfleet), Essex, England.
>
> R.G. Wilson, P.O. Box 54 Greendale Station, Worcester, MA 01606; telephone: (617) 869-2016.
>
> Nick Nicholson Motors, 11629 Van Owen Street, North Hollywood, CA 91605; telephone: (213) 764-8674.

Gringo
> Power-Dyne Vehicles, Inc., Jenks Hills Road, Lincoln, RI 02865; telephone: (401) 728-2900.

Hägglunds
> Sweden

Harley-Davidson
> AMF/Harley-Davidson Motor Co., 3700 West Juneau Avenue, Milwaukee, WI 53201; telephone: (414) 342-4680.

Hodaka
   Pabatco, 327 Sherman Road, Athena, OR 97813; telephone: (503) 566-3526.

   Penartic Distributing Co., Star Route Box 59, Lock Haven, PA 17745; telephone: (717) 769-6482.

   Northeast Hodaka, 17 Main Street, Holden, MA 01520; telephone: (617) 829-3987.

   Tiger Distributing Co., 653 West Broadway, Glendale, CA 91204; telephone: (213) 246-7132.

Holder
   Die Cast Finishing Co., 2020 Lakeside Avenue, Cleveland, OH 44114; telephone: (216) 696-6070.

Honda
   Japan

   American Honda Motor Co., 100 West Alondra Boulevard, P.O. Box 50, Gardena, CA 90247-0805; telephone: (213) 321-8680.

Husqvarna
   Sweden

   Husqvarna East, 1906 Broadway Avenue, Lorain, OH 74051; telephone: (216) 244-1515.

   Husqvarna West, 4935 Mercury Street, San Diego, CA 92111; telephone: (714) 565-1414.

Indian
   Indian Motorcycles, Inc., 110 North Doheny Drive, Beverly Hills, CA 90211; telephone: (213) 278-9470.

Islo
   Grapevine Racing Motors, 750 East Pawnee, Wichita, KS 67211; telephone: (316) 733-1901.

Italjet
   Italy

Izhevsk
   Izhevsk, Russia.

James
   Greet, Birmingham, England.

Jawa
   J. Janacek Arms Manufacturing Co., Prague, Czechoslovakia.

78 / Motorcycle Books

American Jawa, Ltd. 185 Express Street, Plainview, NY 11803; telephone: (516) 938-3210.

American Jawa, Ltd., 18408 Laurel Park Road, Compton, CA 90224; telephone: (213) 537-8400.

Union Sales Distributing Co., 630 North Witchduck Road, Virginia Beach, VA 23462; telephone: (804) 499-8961.

Jupiter
    Izhevsk; Russia.

Kami
    Kami Sales Corporation, 2750-M Oregon Court, Torrance, CA 90503; telephone: (213) 320-3700.

Kawasaki
    Kawasaki Motor Corp. U.S.A., 13 Production Way, Avenel, NJ 07001; telephone (201) 381-0800.

    Kawasaki Motors Corp. U.S.A., 6104 Boat Rock Boulevard, S.W., Atlanta, GA 30336; telephone: (404) 349-2000.

    Kawasaki Motors Corp. U.S.A., 1710 111th Street, Grand Prairie, TX 75050; telephone: (214) 263-5761.

    Kawasaki Motors Corp. U.S.A., 14225 25th Avenue North, Minneapolis, MN 55441; telephone: (612) 546-5341.

    Kawasaki Motors Corp. U.S.A., P.O. Box 25252, Santa Ana, CA 92799-5252; telephone: (714) 540-9980.

Laverda
    Breganze, Italy

    Continental Motorcycles, 150 Ludlow Avenue, Northvale, NJ 07647; telephone: (201) 767-3673.

Maico
    Württemberg, Germany.

    Eastern Maico, Royal and Duke Streets, Reedsville, PA 17084; telephone: (717) 667-3987.

    Debenham Imports, 887 Main Street, Antioch, IL 60002; telephone: (312) 395-2100.

    Cooper Motors, 110 East Santa Ania Avenue, Burbank, CA 91502; telephone: (213) 843-4633.

Manet
    Czechoslovakia

Matchless
   Matchless Motor Cycles Ltd., Plumstead Road, London SE 18, England.

MCB
   Sweden

Monark
   Sweden

   Inter-Trends, 3001 Red Hills Avenue, Costa Mesa, CA 92626; telephone: (714) 979-1550.

Mondial
   Milan, Italy

Montesa
   Permanyer SA, Barcelona, Spain.

   Montesa Motors, Inc., 3657 West Beverly Boulevard, Los Angeles, CA 90004; telephone: (213) 663-8258.

Moto Guzzi
   Moto Guzzi SpA, Mandello del Lario, Italy.

   Premiere Motor Corp., Railroad Street and Plant Road, Hasbrouck Heights, NJ 07604; telephone: (201) 288-9694.

   ZDS Motor Corp., 4655 San Fernando Road, Glendale, CA 91204; telephone: (213) 245-8695.

MV Augusta
   La Meccanica Verghera Augusta.

   Ed LaBelle Cycle Engineering, 15 Calconhood Road, Sharon Hill, PA 19079; telephone: (215) 586-2060.

MZ
   VEB Mottorradwerk, Zschopau, East Germany.

   International Accessories East, 102 Park Street, Hampshire, IL 60140; telephone: (312) 683-3865.

   International Accessories West, 4225 30th Street, San Diego, CA 92104; telephone: (714) 280-3344.

Norman
   Norman Cycles Ltd., Ashford, Kent, England.

Norton
   Norton Motors Limited, Aston, Birmingham 6, and later Plumstead Road, Woolwich, London SE 18, and Norton Villiers Ltd.

Triumph Norton, Inc., 2745 East Huntington Drive, Duarte, CA 91010; telephone: (213) 531-7138.

Berliner Motor Corporation, Railroad Street and Plant Road, Hasbrouck Heights, NJ 07604; telephone: (201) 288-9696.

NSU
NSU Werke AG, Neckarsulm, Germany.

Ossa
Barcelona, Spain.

Yankee Motor Corporation, P.O. Box 36, Schenectady, NY 12306; telephone: (518) 372-4726.

Panther
Phelon and Moore, Yorkshire, England.

Penton
Penton Imports, 3709 West Erie Avenue, Lorain, OH 44053; telephone: (216) 244-4101.

Penton West, 9604 Oates Drive, Sacramento, CA 95827; telephone: (916) 362-4124.

Puch
Austria.

American Puch Distributing Co. East, 148 West Lancaster Avenue, Dowington, PA 19335; telephone: (215) 269-3923.

Puch Distributing Corporation, 9825 Mason Avenue, Chatsworth, CA 91311; telephone: (213) 882-8860.

Rickman
Brothers Engineering Ltd., New Milton, Hampshire, England.

Triumph Norton, Inc., 2745 East Huntington Drive, Duarte, CA 91010; telephone: (213) 531-7138.

Rickman, Inc., 2640 Merchant Drive, Baltimore, MD 21204; telephone: (301) 525-3666.

Rokon
Rokon, Inc., 160 Emerald Street, Keene, NH 03431; telephone: (603) 352-7341.

Royal Enfield
Enfield Cycle Company, England.

Rumi
Moto Rumi, Bergamo, Italy.

Rupp
  Rupp Manufacturing Company, 1776 Airport Road, Mansfield, OH 44903; telephone: (419) 522-5732.

Sparta
  Apeldoorn, Netherlands.

Speedway Sportcycles
  Speedway Products, Inc., 160 East Longview Avenue, Mansfield, OH 44905; telephone: (419) 522-5078.

Sprite
  Sprite Developments Ltd., Halesowen, Worcs., England.

Sunbeam
  Great Britain; flourished 1920-1929; factory bought in 1930 by Imperial Chemical Industries; manufacturing rights sold to BSA in 1943; name and manufacture dropped in 1957.

Suzuki
  Suzuki Motor Company, Hamamatsu, Japan.

  U.S. Suzuki Motor Corporation, 3251 East Imperial Highway, P.O. Box No. 1100; Brea, CA 92622-9988.

  U.S. Suzuki Motor Corporation, 13767 Freeway Drive, Santa Fe Springs, CA 90670; telephone: (213) 921-4461.

Taka
  Rockford Motors, Inc., 1911 Harrison Avenue, Rockford, IL 61108; telephone: (815) 398-1220.

Triumph
  England.

  Triumph Norton, Inc., 2745 East Huntington Drive, Duarte, CA 91010; telephone: (213) 531-7138.

Tyran
  Mitsubishi Corporation, 124 Leuning Street, South Hackensack, NJ 07606; telephone: (201) 342-3600.

Ural
  Russia

Velocette
  Veloce Ltd., Hall Green, Birmingham, England.

Victoria
  Victoria-Werke AG, Nuremberg, Germany.

Vincent-HRD
   England.

Yamaha
   Yamaha Motor Co. Ltd., Japan.

   Yamaha Motor Corporation U.S.A., P.O. Box 6555; Cypress, CA 90630-0500.

Yankee
   Yankee Motor Corporation, P.O. Box 36, Schenectady, NY 12306; telephone: (518) 372-4726.

ZU
   Zweirad Union, Germany.

Zündapp
   Germany.

Mechanics

Construction, Modifications, Maintenance and Service.

Accessory Mart Vintage Catalog. 209p. Catalog for the 1930-1970 British rider. Parts for BSA, Norton, Royal Enfield, and Triumph. Wholesale catalog for Somi Racer.

Alth, Max. All About Motorcycles. 209p. New York: c. 1975. See No. 1.

Annand, and Roe. Gas Flow in the Internal Combustion Engine, Power, Performance, Emission Control and Silencing. 218p, 141 illus, bibliography. 1974.

Arman, Mike. Motorcycle Electrics Without Pain. softbound 64p, 53 photographs and 52 diagrams.

Bacon, R. and Wagner. Electronic Ignition Systems for Cars, Motorcycles and Karts. 52p, 22 illus. c. 1977.

Bacon, Roy. Two-Stroke Carburetion and Ignition. 48p, 15 illus. c. 1969.

_____. Two Stroke Exhaust Systems. 48p, 12 illus. c. 1968.

_____. Two-Stroke Ports for Power. 52p, 21 illus. c. 1968.

_____. Two-Stroke Tuning. 133p, 144 illus.

Bell, A. Graham. Performance Tuning in Theory and Practice: Two Strokes. softbound 7 x 9½" 113 illus.

Bossagilia. Two-Stroke High Performance Engine Design and Tuning. 227p, 250 illus. 1968. British translation from the Italian.

Brierley, Maurice. Supercharging Cars and Motorcycles. 56p, 30 illus. 1966.

British Motorcycle Engines. 8½ x 11" 64p, 65 technical drawings. Los Angeles: Floyd Clymer Publications. Compiled by staff of "Motor Cycle" magazine.

Chilton's Motorcycle Owner's Handbook. 228p, 303 illus. Radnor, PA: Chilton Book Co., c. 1979. Engine functions and maintenance.

Chilton's Motorcycle Repair Manuals. 2nd Edition. 1,200p, 2,500 illus. Radnor, PA: Chilton Book Co., c. 1973. Postwar models of Harley-Davidson, Honda, Kawasaki, Moto Guzzi, Norton, Suzuki, Triumph and Yamaha.

_____. 1974 Edition. 1,376p, 2,500 illus. Radnor, PA: Chilton Book Co., c. 1974. Includes 2nd edition entries in addition to BMW, BSA, Bultaco, Montesa and Ossa.

_____. 1,238p. Radnor, PA: Chilton Book Company, c. 1976.

_____. 1,530p, 3,300 illus. Radnor, PA: Chilton Book Co., c. 1981. Covers Harley-Davidson Singles 1975-76 and V-Twins 1959-76; Honda 4-stroke singles 1968-76, 125-200 Twins 1969-77, 350-360 Twins 1968-77, 450-500 Twins 1966-77, Hawk 1978-81, 750/900 Fours 1969-81, and 350-650 Fours 1972-81; Kawasaki Singles 1969-75, Triples 1969-79, KZ650-750 1976-81, and KZ900/1000 1973-81; Suzuki Singles and Twins 1970-76, Triples 1972-77 and GS 750/850 1977-81; Triumph, all models 1967-74; Yamaha Street 2-strokes 1967-78, XS 360-400 1976-81 and 650 1970-81.

Chilton's Motorcycle Troubleshooting Guide. 165p. Radnor, PA: Chilton Book Co., c. 1973.

_____. 211p, 361 illus. Radnor, PA: Chilton Book Co., c. 1977. Two-stroke and four-stroke.

Clymer, Floyd. Souping Twostroke Engines for More Power and Speed. c. 1968.

Crouse, William H. and Donald L. Anglin. Motorcycle Mechanics. 360p, 540 illus. 1982.

"Cycle World" Road Test Annual 1969. Cycle World Magazine, c. 1969.

Dempsey, Paul. Motorcycle Repair Handbook. 405p. Blue Ridge Summit, PA: c. 1976.

Draper, K.G. The Two-Stroke Engine: Its Design and Tuning. 125p, 40 illus. c. 1968. Tuning your own engine, for motorcyclists, karters, outboard boatmen and others.

Ewers, William. Sincere's Mini-bike Service Book. 132p. Phoenix, AZ: 1971.

Foale, Tony and Vic Willoughby. Motorcycle Chassis Design: The Theory and Practices. softbound 7¼ x 8¼" 160p, 150 illus. c. 1984.

Forsdyke, Graham. Motorcycle Maintenance Illustrated. c. 1969.

Gayler, Bob. Piper Tuning Manual. 44p, 89 illus. 1981. Small 2-strokes to V-12 4-strokes.

Gianatsis, Jim. Design and Tuning for Motocross. 96p, 188 illus.

Griffin, Michael M. Motorcycles From the Inside Out. 239p. Englewood Cliffs, NJ: c. 1978.

Handbook. Motorcycle Overhaul. Pitman, c. 1968.

Holmes, Ron. Motorcycle Science. Denver, CO: c. 1977.

Irving, Phil. Black Smoke. 127p, 83 illus.

_____. Motorcycle Engineering. 330p, 224 illus. Clymer, 1981. Previously published c. 1968 with 179 drawings and photographs with tables in 320p.

_____. Motorcycle Technicalities. 311p, 137 illus. Fifty articles from Motor Cycling, 1930's and early 1940's.

Irving, Philip E. Tuning for Speed. 132 illus. c. 1968, fifth edition.

_____. Twostroke Power Units: The Design and Application. c. 1968.

Jennings, Gordon. Two-Stroke Tuner's Handbook. softbound 156p, 67 illus. Tucson, AZ: c. 1973.

Johns, Bruce A. and David Edmundson. Motorcycles: Fundamentals, Service, Repair. 416p, 1,250 illus. 1983.

Koch, Donald. Chilton's Complete Guide to Motorcycles and Motorcycling. 197p. Radnor, PA: c. 1974. See No. 49.

Lear, George. Motorcycle Mechanics. 266p. Englewood Cliffs, NJ: c. 1977.

Lockwood, Tim. Motorcycle Repair Encyclopedia. 464p, 750 illus. Clymer, c. 1977. This was revised prior to 1977.

Mini-bike Service Manual. 172p. Kansas City, MO: c. 1972.

Minton, David. The Complete Motorcyclist's Handbook. 239p. New York: c. 1981.

Modern Motorcycle Mechanics. Los Angeles: Floyd Clymer Publications.

Moto Guzzi 700, 750 and 850cc Workshop Manual 1967-72. 146p, 175 illus.

Motorcycle and Moped Maintenance. 89p, Secaucus, NJ: c. 1978.

Motorcycle Basics Manual. softbound 8½ x 10½" 164p, 394 illus. c. 1985. "No mechanical knowledge needed." Covers motorcycles, scooters, and mopeds.

Motorcycle Dynamics and Rider Control. 118p, 76 illus.

Motor Cycle Engines Series 1. 64p, 59 illus. Technical articles from Motor Cycle magazine (England) on 24 British engines.

Motorcycle Engineering. Los Angeles: Floyd Clymer Publications.

Motor Cycle Engines Series 2. 64p, 44 illus. Technical articles from Motor Cycle magazine (England) on 16 engines.

Motorcycle Road Tests, 1949-1952. Los Angeles: Floyd Clymer Publications.

Motorcycle Road Tests, 1950-1953. Los Angeles: Floyd Clymer Publications.

"Motor Cycle" Road Tests 1958/59. Motor Cycle (magazine), c. 1968.

Motorcycle Service Manual. 2 volumes. Kansas City, MO: Intertec Pub. Corp., c. 1968. Also c. 1972 and c. 1975.

Motorcycles--How to Manage Them. 320p, 200 illus. Los Angeles: Floyd Clymer Publications and Motor Cycle (magazine), c. 1968.

The Motor Cycling Manual. London: 1902.

"Motor Cycling" Electrical Manual. Motor Cycling (magazine), c. 1968.

"Motor Cycling" Manual. Motor Cycling (magazine), c. 1968.

Motorcycling Manual. 148p, 120 illus. Los Angeles: Floyd Clymer Publications.

"Motor Cycling" Road Tests 7th Series 1962. Motor Cycling (magazine), c. 1968.

"Motor Cycling" Sports Model Road Tests (1938-1959). Motor Cycling (magazine), c. 1968.

The Motorcyclist's Workshop. Los Angeles: Floyd Clymer Publications and Motor Cycle (magazine), c. 1968.

Nicholson, J.B. Modern Motorcycle Mechanics (1945-65). 668p, 500 charts, photographs, data tables, wiring diagrams and assembly drawings. Covers AJS, Ariel, BSA, Harley-Davidson, Honda, Indian, Matchless, Norton, Panther, Parilla, Royal Enfield, Sunbeam, Suzuki, Triumph, Velocette, Villiers, Vincent and Yamaha.

_____. Modern Motorcycle Mechanics, 6th Edition 1939-69. 710p, 312 illus. c. 1969.

Olney, Ross Robert. Light Motorcycle Repair and Maintenance. 65p. New York: c. 1975.

Osborne, Bernal. Modern Motorcycle Maintenance. 245p, illus. 1965.

_____. "Motor Cycling" Electrical Manual. c. 1969.

Petersen's Basic Motorcycles Troubleshooting. 144p, 342 illus. c. 1977. For "owner handy with tools."

Petersen's Motorcycle Repair Manual. 192p, 623 illus. c. 1977. "Fixing problems yourself and handling routine maintenance."

Questions & Answers: Motorcycle Maintenance. 232p, 180 illus. Los Angeles: Floyd Clymer Publications. Also: Motorcyclist (Magazine), c. 1968. Also: 21st edition: 1920-1970. Features Harley-Davidson, Indian, and Mustang. A reprint of the 19th edition, covering 1920-1960. "Invaluable restoration aid."

Richmond, Doug. All About Minibikes. 88p, 100 illus. c. 1977.

Ritch, OCee. Chilton's Italian Motorcycle Repair and Tune-up

Guide. 125p, 200 illus. c. 1977. Covers Aermacchi-Harley, Benelli, Capri, Ducati, Cimatti, Garelli-Rex, Gilera, Italjet, Motobeta, Motobi, Parilla, Riverside, Testi, Zanella motorcycles and Minarelli engines.

_____. Chilton's Motorcycle Troubleshooting Guide. 94p. Philadelphia: c. 1966.

Schoemark, Pete. Motorcycle Carburettor Manual. 117p, 237 illus. Covers Mukuni, Keihin, Amal, Bendix and SU types.

Schultz, Neil. The Complete Guide to Motorcycle Repair and Maintenance. 213p. Garden City, NY: c. 1977. Also: 215p, c. 1980 edition.

Siposs, George G. Building and Racing Radio Control Cars and Motorcycles. 176p, 80 illus.

Shipman, Carl. Motorcycle Tuning for Performance. softbound, 174p, 175 illus. c. 1977.

Small Motorcycle Service Manual. 144p. Kansas City, MO: c. 1974.

Smith, LeRoi Tex. Fixing Up Motorcycles. 202p. New York: c. 1974. See No. 93.

Smith, Phillip. The High Speed Two-Stroke Petrol Engine. c. 1969.

_____ and John Morrison. Scientific Design of Exhaust and Intake Systems. 274p, 200 illus. Third edition, c. 1977.

_____. The High Speed Twostroke Petrol Engine. c. 1968.

_____. The Scientific Design of Exhaust and Intake Systems. 274p, Cambridge, MA: c. 1971.

Souping Two-Stroke Engines for More Power and Speed. Los Angeles: Floyd Clymer Publications. c. 1969. Five articles from Clymer's Motor Cycle magazine.

Speed and Sport. Two Wheeler Care. c. 1970.

Speed--How To Obtain It. 192p. Los Angeles: Floyd Clymer Publications and Motor Cycle (magazine), c. 1968. Includes twostroke.

Thiffault, Mark. Motorcycle Digest.

Tranter, A. Haynes Motorcycle Electrical Manual. 125p, illus.

Two-Stroke Cycle Spark-Ignition Engines. 457p, 588 illus.

Two-Stroke Motorcycles and How to Get the Best from Them. 80 line drawings. Los Angeles: Floyd Clymer Publications and Motor Cycle (magazine), c. 1968. Covers AMC, Villiers, including Starmaker, BSA, Bantam and H-D 2-strokes, Suzuki, Yamaha, MZ, Ariel 119, Royal-Enfield, Lucas alternator and electrics.

Unofficial Flat Rate Manual for Harley Davidson Motorcycles. 24p.

Vierdag, J.W. Improving Twostroke Engine Performance. c. 1968.

Willoughby, Vic. Back to Basics. 120p, 154 illus.

Yerkow, Charles. Motorcycles: How They Work. 95p. New York: c. 1971.

Racing

Abraham, Ian and Colin Irwin. Speedway Spectacular. 32p, 42 illus, 12 in color. Oval dirt-track racing; only partially about motorcycles.

Archer, Leslie. Scrambles and Motorcross. c. 1968.

Bacon, Roy. Foreign Racing Motorcycles. hardbound 7 x 9½" 204p, 14 illus. One-hundred racing motorcycles from Europe and Japan.

_____. Taking Up Motorcycle Racing. c. 1968.

Bailey, Gary. Gary Bailey's How to Win Motocross. 190p. Tucson, AZ: c. 1974.

_____ with Carl Shipman. How to Win Motocross. 190p, 200 illus. Tucson, AZ: c. 1974. From the Gary Bailey motocross school.

Booth, Steve and Brian Palormo. Championship Enduro. softbound, 128p, 203 photographs. Preparation and competition.

Bula, Maurice. Grand Prix Motorcycle Championships of the World 1949-1975. 300p, 350 illus. c. 1977.

Carrick, Peter. Encyclopaedia of Motor-Cycle Sport. 240p, 40 photographs. 1982 (second edition). Road-racing. See No. 14.

_____. Motorcycle Racing. 260 illus. c. 1969. See No. 14.

Carter, Chris. Motocourse 1976-1977. hardbound 200p, 300 photographs, 24 in color. c. 1977. First edition of this annual; first issue.

_____. Motocourse 1977-78. hardbound 200p, 300 photographs, 24 in color. c. 1978. Second issue.

Cathcart, Alan. Classic Motorcycle Racer Tests. hardbound 7½ x 8½" 192p, 160 illus. Twenty track tests of postwar road racing classics.

Clew, Jeff. British Racing Motorcycles. hardbound 183p, 50 illus. c. 1977.

Clifford, Peter. The Art and Science of Motorcycle Racing. hardbound 284p, 100 illus, 20 in color. 1985. Foreword by Eddie Lawson. See No. 20.

_____. Motocourse 1982-83. hardbound 9½ x 12¼" 200p, 300 illus, 50 in color. c. 1983. See No. 21.

_____. Motocourse 1984-85. 192p, 200 illus, 50 color photographs.

Motocourse 1985-1986. 9½ x 12-3/4" 192p, 220 illus, 50 in color. 1986. Tenth edition of this annual. See No. 22.

Code, Keith. A Twist of the Wrist: The Motorcycle Road Racer's Handbook. softbound 8¼ x 10½" 117p, 72 illus. c. 1983.

Competition Yearbook. Floyd Clymer Publications. Motorcycling News, 1962.

Coonfield, Ed. Enduro Secrets Revealed. 176p, 53 illus. Preparation and competition. See No. 24.

Davison, G.S. Motorcycle Road Racing: Isle of Man Tourist Trophy History. 189p.

Deane, Charles. Isle of Man TT. hardbound 152p, 73 illus. c. 1977. First 30 years from 1907 and postwar races.

Dixon, Alan. The TT Riders. c. 1968.

Ekins, Bud, and Johnny McLaughlin, and Chuck "Feets" Minert and Don Pink. How to Ride and Win. 116p.

Engel, Lyle Kenyon. Off-road Racing. 148p. New York: c. 1974.

European Motorcycling in Two Volumes. Grass Track. 32p. c. 1970.

_____. Racing Champions. 32 p. c. 1970.

Foster, Gerald. Ride It! The Complete Book of Flat Track Racing. 155p, 148 illus.

Gianatsis, Jim. Design and Tuning for Motocross. 96p, 188 illus.

Grass Track. Motor Cycle News, c. 1968.

Griffin, Mike. Motorcycle Drag Racing. 125p, 300 illus. Preparation and practice.

Hailwood, Mike. The Art of Motorcycle Racing. 80 photographs. c. 1970.

Hatfield, Jerry. American Racing Motorcycles. 224p, 143 photographs.

How to Ride and Win. Los Angeles: Floyd Clymer Publications.

Jones, Thomas Firth. Enduro Handbook. Chilton Publishers.

King, Max. Trials Riding. c. 1968.

Lackey, Brad and Len Weed. Motocross: Techniques, Training and Tactics. softbound, 226p, 430 illus.

Lanning, Dave. Speedway and Short Track Racing. 128p. London, New York: c. 1974.

Leavitt, Lane and Len Weed. Motor Cycle Trials: Techniques and Training. 160p, 400 illus.

Louis, John. A Secondary Look Inside Speedway. 144p, 100 illus. c. 1977. Competition and mechanical developments.

Main-Smith, Bruce. The First Post-Vintage Racing Scene (1931-1951). 64 p, 115 illus.

_____. The First Vintage Racing (Pre-1931). 64p, 100 illus. c. 1977.

Mallet, David and John Imre. The Canyon Racer's Pocket Guide to Advanced Motorcycling Techniques. softbound 4 x 8½" 80p. Interview with Steve Baker.

Mauger, Ivan and Peter Oakes. Ivan Mauger's Speedway Extravaganza No. 1. 112p, 100 photographs, 17 in color. c. 1977.

_____. Ivan Mauger's Speedway Extravaganza No. 2. 112p, 140 photographs, 7 in color. c. 1977.

May, Cyril. Ride It! The Complete Book of Speedway. 156p, 132 illus. c. 1977.

McKinnon, Andrew. Motorcycle Road Racing in the Fifties. 160p, 150 illus.

Motorcycle Engines: Famous British Designs Analysed. Motor Cycle (magazine), c. 1968.

Melling, Frank. Enduro Motorcycles. softbound 144p, 120 illus, 17 in color. Track tests of off-road bikes, including Fantic, SWM, Kawasaki, Yamaha, Suzuki, KTM, Honda, Jawa, Moto-Gori, Montesa, Husqvarna, Maico, CCM and BMW.

_____. Motocross: The Big Leap. 168p, 123 illus, 14 color photographs.

_____. Ride It! The Complete Book of Motocross. 157p, 140 illus. c. 1977.

Miller, D. and L. Weed. Championship Training. softbound 8½ x 11" 112p, 91 illus. Also with tips from Brad Lackey.

Miller, Sammy. Clean to the Finish. 72p, 210 illus. How to ride trials.

Morley, Don. Classic British Trials Bikes. 192p, 165 illus. Osprey Collector's Library, c. 1984. Covers all pre-1965 four-stroke trials bikes, AJS through Velocette.

Moss, Stirling and Mike Hailwood. Racing and All That. 155p, 26 illus. See No. 62.

Motocourse. hardbound, 200p, 300 illus, 50 in color. 1981-82. Also see: Clifford Peter and Carter, Chris.

Motor Cycle News. Moto Cross. c. 1970.

1977 Motorcycle Racing Annual. 224p, 350 photographs, 240 in color. c. 1977.

Motorcycle Racing Champions. 95p. New York: c. 1975.

Motorcycle Road Racing. Los Angeles: Floyd Clymer Publications. Isle of Man.

Murray, Jerry. The Handbook of Motocross. 118p. New York: c. 1978.

Mutch, Ronnie. The Last of the Great Road Races. 135p, 58 illus. c. 1977. Isle of Man Tourist Trophy races.

Patrick, Mike. Focus on Speedway. 96p, 50 illus, 24 in color. c. 1977.

_____. Mike Patrick's Speedway Scene. 96p, 149 photographs, 12 in color. c. 1977.

Patrignani, Roberto and C. Perelli. Color Treasury of Motorcycle Competition. 64p, 130 illus, 79 in color. See No. 67.

Patrignani, Roberto. Motorcycle Competition. 64p. New York: c. 1974.

Perry, Robin. The Trials Motorcyclist. 152p. New York: c. 1975.

Pickard, Derek. British 250 Racer. 72p, 113 illus. Development of the Greeves Silverstone, with additional material on Villiers, Cotton, Royal Enfield, Alpha, Ariel AJS and others.

Racing Champions and Challengers. Motor Cycle News, c. 1968.

The Racing Game. Floyd Clymer Publications.

Radlauer, Edward. Scramble Cycle. 47p. New York: c. 1971.

Redman, Jim. Wheels of Fortune. c. 1970.

Robinson, John. Ride It! The Complete Book of Endurance Racing. 159p, 150 illus.

Sammy Miller on Trials. c. 1970.

Schreiber, Bernie and Len Weed. Observed Trials. Advice on technique.

Scramble: Men and Machines in Motocross. Motor Cycle News, c. 1968.

Shipman, Carl. How to Ride Observed Trials Just for Fun! softbound 158p, 278 photographs. Tucson, AZ: c. 1973. Selection, modification and skills with trial bikes.

Silver and Douglas. The Speedway Annual. c. 1969.

Sixty Years of Speed. Motor Cycle News, c. 1968.

Smith, Don. Ride It! The Complete Book of Motorcycle Trials. 132p, 155 illus. c. 1977.

_____. Trials Bike Riding. 112p. East Ardsley, England: c. 1980.

Smith, Jeff. The Art of Motocross. c. 1969.

_____. Jeff Smith on Scrambling. c. 1968.

Smith, Philip H. The Greatest of All Trials. The Scott Motorcycle Trials 1914-37. c. 1969.

Surtees, John. John Surtees on Racing. c. 1968.

Swift, Jim. Ride It! The complete Book of Big Bike Racing. 149p, 175 illus. c. 1977.

TT Action 1967. Motor Cycle News, c. 1968.

Thiffault, Mark. Motorcycle Digest. See No. 99.

Whyte, Norris. Motorcycle Racing Champions. 96p, 121 illus, 21 in color. 1975. See No. 106.

Willoughby, Vic. The Racing Motorcycle. 176p, 250 illus, 17 in color. Technical development, races and riders.

Woollett, Mick. Racing Motor Cycles. 96p. London, New York: c. 1980. See No. 114.

_____. Speedbikes. 65p, 40 color photographs. Twenty-nine racing bikes.

_____. World Championship Motorcycle Racing. 128p, 161 illus, 109 in color.

Wright, Stephen. American Racing 1900-1940. 11¼ x 12½" 250p, 281 illus. England, Australia and New Zealand. See No. 116.

Zonker, Patricia. Murdercycles. 204p, 10p illus. Chicago: c. 1978.

Reference

Accessory Mart Vintage Catalog. 109p. Catalog for the 1930-1970 British rider. Parts on BSA, Norton, Royal Enfield and Triumph. Wholesale catalog for Domi Racer.

Albion Scott-Motobooks, 48 East 50th Street, New York, NY 10022.

Christensen, Richard D. Motorcycles in Magazines. 350p, 9 illus. Chronological list, 1895-1983. See No. 18.

Classic Motorbooks, P.O. Box 1, 729 Prospect Avenue, Osceola, WI 54020; 715-924-3345; Books by mail: 1-800-826-6600.

Kosbab, William. Motorcycle Dictionary/Terminology. softbound 5¼ x 8½" 363p. c. 1985.

The Motorcyclists Encyclopedia. 64p, 140 illus. c. 1977. 2200 terms.

Motorcycle Statistical Annual. Newport Beach, CA. 1977.

Oakes, Peter and Ivan Mauger. Speedway Quiz Book No. 1. 128p, 80 illus. c. 1977. Sports records.

R. Gordon, 12 East 55th Street, New York, NY 10022. Bookstore.

Vivian Gray, Hurstpierpoint, Sussex, England. Mail-order motor bookseller.

Williams, P.M. Motorcycle Data Book (1946-60). c. 1968.

Restoration

The Art of Custom Painting. 64p, 368 illus. c. 1977.

Bacon, Roy. Triumph Twin Restoration. hardbound 7½ x 11" 240p, 200 illus. c. 1985. A guide for restoring pre-1972 production twins.

Bird, Dick. The Art of Freehand Pinstriping. 66p, 200 illus.

Clew, Jeff. The Restoration of Vintage and Thoroughbred Motorcycles. hardbound 208p, 282 illus. Phoenix, AZ: c. 1977.

Egan, M.F. M.F. Egan's Vintage Motorcycle Parts Catalog. 160p, 800 illus. Harley-Davidson and Indian.

Irving, Phil. Restoring and Tuning Classic Motor Cycles. 80p, 192 illus.

Page, Victor, W. Early Motorcycles: Construction, Operation, Service. 512p, 300 illus.

Revere, Paul. Do Your Own Motor-Bike Spraying and Customizing. 96p, 225 illus, 4 in color.

Riding

Alth, Max. Motorcycles and Motorcycling. 90p. New York: c. 1979. See No. 2.

Cunningham, Chet. Your Bike. 126p. New York: c. 1975.

Cutter, Robert Arthur. The New Guide to Motorcycling. 159p. New York: c. 1974. See No. 26.

Davis and McCarthy. Ride ... And Stay Alive. 120p, 58 illus. Motorcycle safety.

Ditchburn, Blackett. Superbiking: A Manual for Fast Street

Riding. softbound 128p, 100 illus. Photographs by Don Morely.

_____. Superbiking. softbound 128p, 100 illus. On fast street biking. See No. 28.

Domokos, Doug. Wheelyin' With the King. 144p, 300 illus, 12 in color. Basic "wheeling" and varieties of tricks.

Edmonds, I.G. Motorcycling for Beginners. 156p. Philadelphia: c. 1972.

Felsen, Henry Gregor. Living With Your First Motorcycle. 94p. New York: c. 1976.

Forsdyke, Graham. Off Road Motor Cycle Sport. 156p. London: 1976.

Gutkind, Lee. Bike Fever. 233p. Chicago: c. 1973. See No. 39.

Hampton, William. Expert Motorcycling. 151p. Chicago: c. 1979.

Harris, Maz. Bikers: Birth of a Modern Day Outlaw. softbound 8½ x 9-3/4" 128p, 139 photographs. See No. 42.

Hints and Tips for Motorcyclists, Scooter and Noped Riders. Motor Cycle (magazine), c. 1968.

How to Organize a Motorcycle Club. Los Angeles: Floyd Clymer Publications.

How to Ride a Motorcycle. 56p. Los Angeles: Floyd Clymer Publications.

Hudson-Evans, Richard. Handbook of Motorcycle Sport. 144p. New York: c. 1978.

Huetter, John. Motorcycling U.S.A. 120p. New York: c. 1977.

Jackson, Bob. Street Bike Fun. 175p. Tucson, AZ: 1975. See No. 47.

Kaysing, William. Fell's Beginner's Guide to Motorcycling. 256p. New York: c. 1976.

Koch, Donald. Chilton's Complete Guide to Motorcycles and Motorcycling. 197p. Radnor, PA: c. 1974. See No. 49.

Lyon, Danny. The Bikeriders. 94p. New York: 1967. See No. 54.

96 / Motorcycle Books

Manners for Motorcyclists. Floyd Clymer Publications.

Main-Smith, Bruce. The Book of Super Bike Road Tests. 64p, 200 illus. c. 1977. Larger bikes (1,200cc Harley-Davidson and 1,000cc Vincent).

Melling, Frank. Ride It! The Complete Book of Trail Bike Riding. 135p, 150 illus. c. 1977.

Motorcycle Road Craft. 88p, 49 illus. c. 1968. Edited by British police riders.

Motorcyclist's Magazine Dirt Bike Guide. 96p, 211 illus. Petersen series.

Perry, Robin. The Road Rider. 152p. New York: c. 1974. See No. 69.

_____. The Woods Rider. 144p. New York: c. 1973. See No. 70.

Radlauer, Edward. Motorcycle Mutt. 48p. New York: c. 1973.

Richmond, Doug. How to Select, Ride and Maintain Your Trail Bike. 160p, 175 illus. Tucson, AZ: c. 1972.

Roth, Bernhard A. The Complete Beginner's Guide to Motorcycling. 174p. Garden City, NY: c. 1974.

Salinger, Peter H. Motorcycling and the New Enthusiast. 95p. New York: c. 1973. See No. 80.

Shipman, Carl. The Boonie Book. 189p, 200 illus. c. 1977 (2nd edition). Dirt riding.

Streano, Vince. Touching America With Two Wheels. 139p. New York: c. 1974. See No. 96.

Thiffault, Mark. Motorcycle Digest. 21 x 28cm (8½ x 11") ppw, 320 illus. Chicago, Follett Publishing Co., 1972. See No. 99.

Wallach, Theresa. Easy Motorcycle Riding. 144p. New York: 1970. See No. 105

Williamson, Mitch. Safe Riding. 224p. New York: c. 1980. See No. 108.

Yeager, Trisha. How To Be Sexy With Bugs In Your Teeth. 176p. Chicago: c. 1978.

Yerkow, Charles. Fun and Safety on Two Wheels. 142p. New York: c. 1979.

Travel and Touring

Around the World with Motorcycle and Camera. Floyd Clymer Publications.

Boswell, Cliff and George Hays. Two-Wheel Touring and Camping. Bagnall Publishing Co., 1969. Supplies addresses for travel information and statistics on National Parks with specific chapters on tenting, and on Mexico. See No. 7.

Craven, Ken. Ride It! The Complete Book of Motorcycle Touring. 135p, 174 illus. c. 1977. See No. 25.

Huetter, John. Motorcycling U.S.A. 120 p. New York: c. 1977.

Kolb, Hazel and Bill Stermer. On the Perimeter. 227p. Touring the perimeter of the United States.

Lovin, Roger. The Complete Motorcycle Nomad. 308p. Boston: c. 1974. See No. 53.

Philcox. Phil and Beverly Boe. How To Tour Europe by Motorcycle. 138p, 80 illus.

Stermer, Bill. Motorcycle Touring. 144p, 263 illus, 60 in color. Preparations.

Thoeming, Peter and Peter Rae. Motorcycle Touring. 191p, 125 illus, 14 in color. Europe and United States experiences.

Two Wheel Travel: Motorcycle Camping and Touring. 125p. New Canaan, CT: c. 1972.

Video

Against the Odds. On Jarno Saarinen. 65 minutes. VHS and Beta.

American Challenge. 1982 Belgian GP with Freddie Spencer and Steve Baker in the 1978 600 and 750 World Championships. 65 minutes. VHS and Beta.

Austrian Bike Grand Prix 1985. VHS and Beta.

Austrian Enduro. 1981 Austrian Round of the European 2-day Enduro Championship. Also features <u>Trials and Tribulations</u>, motor cycle trials riding set to music, and <u>Motocross Masters</u>, on the 1981 British Motocross Championship. 62 minutes. VHS and Beta.

Belgian Bike Grand Prix 1985. VHS and Beta.

British Bike Grand Prix 1985. VHS and Beta.

98 / Motorcycle Books

Daytona 1983 Superbike and Supercross Race. 53 minutes. VHS and Beta.

Daytona 1983 200 Classic Race. 53 minutes. VHS and Beta.

Donnington World Cup 82. Mamola, Haslam, Ballington, others. 55 minutes. VHS.

Dutch Bike Grand Prix 1985. VHS and Beta.

Easy Rider. Peter Fonda. 84 minutes. VHS and Beta.

Enduro International. Covers 1983 International Six Days Enduro at Buith Wells, Wales. 60 minutes. VHS and Beta.

French Bike Grand Prix 1985. VHS and Beta.

German Bike Grand Prix 1985. VHS and Beta.

Grand Prix 1956. TT Sidecar Race at Clypse, TT 500cc, Ulster GP 350cc, Ulster GP Sidecar and Ulster GP 500cc. 53 minutes. VHS.

Honda: The Technology. Late 1982 technology, tests and demonstrations. VHS and Beta.

The Island. 1980 Isle of Man TT races. 43 minutes VHS and Beta.

Italian Bike Grand Prix 1985. VHS and Beta.

Italian Finale. 1983 500cc World Road Race Championship at Imola with Freddie Spencer, Kenny Roberts, Marco Lucchinelli and Eddie Lawson. 45 minutes. VHS and Beta.

Lone Champion Video. Features Freddie Spencer, Randy Mamola, Ray Roche, Barry Sheene, others. Covers 1984 season. 60 minutes. VHS and Beta.

Making of a Champion. With Freddie Spencer and the 1983 world championship. 22 minutes. VHS and Beta.

Motocross Professionals. 1978-79 GP in France, Italy and Belgium. 62 minutes. VHS and Beta.

Narrow Edge. Grand Prix racing 1974 with Giacomo Agostini and Barry Sheene and Phil Read. 65 minutes. VHS and Beta.

Off Road Action. Top trial riders. Also sidecar action. With Brad Lackey, in France. 64 minutes. VHS and Beta.

On Any Sunday. Mexican 1000 off-track trials race. 89 minutes VHS and Beta.

On Any Sunday II. With Bruce Penhall, Brad Lackey, Bob Hannah and Kenny Roberts. 89 minutes. VHS and Beta.

Race to the Top. 1977 Dutch TT and 1981 Race of the Year. Sheene, Mamola, Crosby and Herron. 65 minutes. VHS and Beta.

Racing Into History. Racing from late 1950's and early 1960's. Includes 1959 Silverston, 1959 Oulton and Oulton Sidecar race, and 1962 Oulton championship and 1958 Isle of Man TT sidecar and senior races. 53 minutes. VHS.

San Marino Bike Grand Prix 1985. VHS and Beta.

Scrambling in the Fifties. 1955 Victory Trial from Church Stretton; 1956 Experts Grand National from Rosewood Park; 1956 Sunbeam Point-to-Point from Tattingham Park; 1956 Lancashire Grand National from Cuerden Park; 1958 Sunbeam Point-to-point; 1959 Cotswold Scramble from Petersfield. 50 minutes. VHS and Beta.

Silverstone 83. 1983 500, 125 and 250 and sidecar races with interviews with Spencer, Roberts, Sheene, Mamola and Haslam. 60 minutes. VHS and Beta.

South African Bike Grand Prix 1985. VHS and Beta.

Spanish Bike Grand Prix 1985. VHS and Beta.

Speedway 82. Los Angeles, with Kenny Carter and Bruce Penhall. 78 minutes. VHS and Beta.

Superbowl '75: Motocross. Los Angeles Coliseum with Jimmy Ellis. 28 minutes. VHS and Beta.

Superstar Showdown: 1984 Transatlantic Challenge. Donnington Park, GP and unlimited superbikes. 48 minutes. VHS.

Swedish Bike Grand Prix 1985. VHS and Beta.

Take it to the Limit. Many forms of motorcycle racing. 95 minutes. VHS and Beta.

TT Tribute. Features Mike Hailwood up to 1979. 69 minutes. VHS and Beta.

V Four Victory. Isle of Man as seen from Joey Dunlop's bike. Also Ulster Grand Prix. 54 minutes. VHS and Beta.

Yugoslavian Bike Grand Prix 1985. VHS and Beta.

Part III

SUPPLEMENTARY LIST OF BOOKS, CATALOGS, AND HANDBOOKS ON MOTORCYCLES BY MAKE

When available the author is listed by last name, followed by the title, description of the book, and, finally, place, publisher, and date of publication. "c." (for circa) indicates only that the book was available to the public in that year, but may have been technically out of print in regard to the publisher's stock. A comment on the contents may conclude a particular listing.

ACE (American)

Ace 4- Cylinder Sales Catalog. 8 x 10½ 15p, 16 illus. c. 1986.

AJS (British)

AJS and Matchless Single and Twin Spares List. 56p, 30 illus. c. 1986. Covers the 1956 350cc 16 MS, 16 MCT, 16 MCS 500cc, 18S, and 1958 16MS, 16CT, 16CS, 500cc 18S, 20, 600cc 30, 30CS.

AJS and Matchless Single Motorcycles 1957-66 Shop Manual. 125p, 38 illus. c. 1986. Covers 1958-1964 Lightweight 250cc and 350cc models G2, G2S, G2CSR, 14, 14S, 14CS, 14CSR, G5, 8 and 1957 to 1966 heavyweight 350cc, 500cc and 600cc models G3, G3C, G3S, G3LS, G3LCS, G80, G80S, G80CS, TCS, 16, 16S, 16C, 16CS, 16MC, 16MCS, 18, 18S, and 18CS.

Bacon, Roy. AJS and Matchless: The Postwar Models. 192p, 165 illus. Osprey Collector's Library, 1983. Covers lightweight singles and twins from 1945.

Grant, Gregor. AJS: The History of a Great Motorcycle. hardbound 112p, 85 illus. 1969. 1897 to recent times.

Haycraft. AJS Singles. Models 1955-65, 350cc and 500cc.

Main-Smith, Bruce. The First AMC Racing Scene. softbound, 64p, 126 photographs. c. 1986. Postwar Matchless and AJS racing machines.

Neill, F.W. AJS and Matchless Twins Workshop Manual 1955-65. Lodgemark, c. 1969.

1935 AJS Owner's Manual. 28p, 2 illus. c. 1986.

AJS 350/500 Singles Handbook 1955-65. Pitman, c. 1968.

Service and Overhaul Manual for the AJS and Matchless Twin Motorcycles. 88p, 34 illus. c. 1986. Covers all 1955 to 1965 models including the AJS G9, G9CS, G9CSR, G11, G11CS, G12, G12CS, G12CSR; Matchless 20, 20CS, 20CSR, 30, 30CS, 31, 31CS and 31CSR.

ARIEL (British)

Ariel Single Handbook 1939-58. Pitman, c. 1968. Leader/Arrow 250 Twins 1958-64.

1939-48 Ariel Square Four Owner's Manual. 4 x 6¼" 56p, 18 illus. c. 1986.

Bacon, Roy. Ariel: The Postwar Models. 192p, 165 illus. Osprey Collector's Library, 1983. Covers the square 4 and light and heavyweight singles and twins from 1945.

Harper, Roy. Ariel Square Four Super Profile. 56p, 94 illus, 18 in color. c. 1986. Evolution from prototype to last production model of the Ariel Square Four.

Haycraft. Ariel. Models 1939-59.

Main-Smith, Bruce. The First Classic Ariel Scene. 64p, 124 illus. c. 1986. Post World-War II models.

Waller, C.W. Ariel Maintenance and Repair Manual 1933-51. Los Angeles: Clymer, c. 1969.

_____. Ariel Owner's Handbook. 200p, 70 photographs, charts, drawings. Los Angeles: Clymer. Maintenance and repair of single-cylinder, twin-cylinder, and four-cylinder models.

_____. Maintenance and Repair Manual. Pearson, c. 1968. All models 1948-60.

Ariel Leader and Arrow Twins Handbook 1958-65. Pitman, c. 1968.

MV AUGUSTA (Italian)

Carrick, Peter. The Story of MV Augusta Motor Cycles. 128p. Cambridge, England: c. 1979.

Clew, Jeff. MV Augusta 750S America Super Profile. 56p, 61 photographs, 19 in color. c. 1986.

BMW (Bavarian Motor Works)

Bacon, Roy. BMW Twins and Singles. hardbound 7½ x 8½" 200p, 150 illus. Osprey Collector's Library, 1982. Also printed with 191p, 166 illus. Covers postwar 250, 450, 500, 600, 650, 750, 800, 900 and 1000cc models.

BMW Motorcycle Shop Manual and Handbook. 275p, 400 photographs, charts, drawings. Los Angeles: Clymer, c. 1969. All models singles and twins. Also listed as "All models 1956-57."

Clymer BMW Service, Repair Handbook. 17.8 x 25.4 cm (7 x 10"). Los Angeles: Clymer, c. 1986.

    BMW Twins. 162p, 330 illus. Covers 500 and 600cc, 1955-69.

    BMW Twins. 264p, 545 illus. Covers 600-900cc, 1955-1975.

    BMW Twins. 206p, 373 illus. Covers 500-1000cc.

Croucher, Robert. The Story of BMW Motor Cycles. 128p, 126 illus. c. 1986.

Frostick, Michael. BMW, The Bavarian Motor Works. 208p, 325 illus. 1976. Thirty pages feature the motorcycles; 62 photographs.

Harper, Roy. BMW R69 and R69S. 56p, 86 illus, 20 in color. c. 1986.

Haynes BMW Twins, 1970; Owner's Workshop Manual. 133p, 346 illus. c. 1986. Covers 498, 599, 746 and 898cc models. Also issued with 170p, 408 illus, 1970-83.

Knittel, Stefan. BMW Motorrader.

Setright, L.J.K. Barnstormer: The Story of BMW Motorcycles. hardbound 190p, 100 illus. c. 1977. 1923 to c. 1977.

Verlag, Ariel. BMW: Motorrader Typen und Technik. hardbound 180p, 325 illus. c. 1977. Technical development; French, German and English text.

BRIDGESTONE (Japanese)

Clymer Bridgestone Owner's Handbook. 84p, 134 illus. Los Angeles: Clymer, c. 1968. Covers 50, 60, 90 and 175cc, 1967. Also listed for years 1967-69, published c. 1969.

BROUGH SUPERIOR (British)

Clark, Ronald H. Brough Superior: The Rolls-Royce of Motorcycles. 176p, 102 photographs. c. 1968. History covering 1920s and 1930s.

Simms, Colin. Brough Superior SS100 Super Profile. 56p, 130 illus, 20 in color. History of this model.

BSA (Birmingham Small Arms)

Bacon, Roy. BSA Gold Star and Other Singles. 192p, 164 illus. Osprey Collector's Library, c. 1986. Covers the postwar Gold Star, B, M, and C. Foreword by Brian Martin.

_____. BSA Twins and Triples. hardbound 7½ x 8½" 160p, 150 illus. Osprey Collector's Library, c. 1986. Also printed in 191p, 165 illus. Foreword by Bob Currie. Covers postwar A7/A10, A50/65 and Rocket 3.

BSA Bantam Handbook 1948-66. Pitman, c. 1968.

BSA Bantam Owner's Manual. 53p, 24 illus. c. 1986. Covers D1 125cc Competition, D3 150cc Bantam Major, D3 150cc Competition. c. 1986.

BSA D/14/4 1968-69. c. 1969.

BSA Motorcycles 1935-40. Temple Press, c. 1969.

BSA Gold Star. hardbound 8½ x 11" 56p, 90 illus, 20 in color. From prototype to last production model, with opinions, tests, specifications.

BSA M20 and M21. hardbound 8½ x 11" 56p, 90 illus, 20 in color. From prototype to last production model, with opinions, tests, specifications.

BSA Super Profiles. hardbound 8½ x 11" 56p, 90 illus, 20 in color. c. 1985.

Chilton's BSA Repair and Tune-up Guide. 17.8 x 26.1 cm (7 x 10¼") 176p, 249 illus. c. 1977. Covers all unit-construction models through 1972.

Clew, Jeff. BSA Bantam Super Profile. 56p, 90 illus, 20 in color. c. 1986. Evolution from prototype to last production model.

Clymer BSA Service, Repair Handbook. softbound 17.8 x 25.4 cm (7 x 10") 164p, 244 illus. Los Angeles: Clymer, c. 1977. Covers 500 and 650cc.

The Gold Star Book. softbound 138p, 174 illus. c. 1977. Workshop manual with development history of post-war years. Covers models ZB, BB, CB, DB, DBD 350 and 500cc machines.

BSA 250 Singles Handbook 1954-66. Pitman, c. 1968. Also issued covering 1954-68.

BSA 350/500 Singles Handbook 1955-64. Pitman, c. 1968. Also issued covering 1955-67.

BSA, Sunbeam and Triumph Tigress Handbook 1959-65. Pitman, c. 1969.

BSA Twins Handbook 1948-62. Pitman, c. 1968.

BSA A50/65 Workshop Manual 1965. c. 1968.

BSA A50/A65 Workshop Manual 1966. c. 1968.

BSA B44 Workshop Manual 1966. c. 1968.

BSA D10 Workshop Manual 1967. c. 1968.

BSA B44/B25/C25 Workshop Manual 1967. c. 1968.

BSA All Models Workshop Manual 1945-68. c. 1968.

Golland, A. Goldie. 79p, 71 illus. c. 1986. Development history of Gold Star BSA.

Haycraft. BSA Singles. Models 1955-64. Four-stroke singles.

Haycraft. BSA Twins. Pitman, c. 1969. Models 1948-62.

Haynes BSA Owner's Workshop Manual. softbound 27.3 x 21 cm (10-3/4 x 8¼") 144p, 310 illus. c. 1977. Covers A50 and A65 series through 1973. Also issued in 88p, 211 illus. c. 1986.

Haynes BSA Pre-unit Singles Owner's Workshop Manual. softbound 27.3 x 21 cm (10-3/4 x 8¼") 144p, 310 illus. c. 1977. Covers 348, 496, 499 and 591cc, 1954 to 1961.

Haynes BSA Singles Owner's Workshop Manual. softbound 27.3 x 21 cm (10-3/4 x 8¼") 118p, 225 illus. c. 1977. Covers 250, 350, 440 and 500 United through 1973.

Haynes BSA A7 and A10 Twins Owner's Workshop Manual. softbound 27.3 x 21 cm (10-3/4 x 8¼") 127p, 243 illus. c. 1977. Covers 497, 646cc 1947 to approximately 1977. All 305 illus in c. 1986 issue.

Holliday, Bob. The Story of BSA Motorcycles. 128p, 80 illus. c. 1986.

Lupton. BSA 250. Models 1954-62.

Main-Smith, Bruce. BSA Motorcycles 1935 to 1940. 70p, 59 illus. Bruce Main-Smith, c. 1977. Technical data and roadtests. All roadster models 149 to 986cc.

_____. The First Classic BSA Scene. softbound 64p. 1938 to 1972 models.

Ryerson, Barry. The Giants of Small Heath: The History of BSA. hardbound 190p, 137 illus. c. 1986. History of the company from the 1910 motor-bicycle.

Wright, Owen. BSA A7 and A10 Twins Super Profile. 56p, 130 illus, 20 in color. c. 1986. Evolution from prototype to last production model. Also roadtests, purchasing and clubs.

BULTACO (Spanish)

Clymer Bultaco Service, Repair Handbook. softbound 17.8 x 25.4 cm (7 x 10") 190p, 298 illus. Los Angeles: Clymer, c. 1977.

Haynes Bultaco Competition Bikes Owner's Workshop Manual. softbound 27.3 x. 21 cm (10-3/4 x 8¼") 92p, 187 illus. c. 1977. Covers Alpina, Frontera, Pursang, Sherpa T 1972 to c. 1977.

CZ (Czechoslovakian)

Clymer CZ Service, Repair Handbook. softbound 17.8 x 25.4 cm (7 x 10") 132p, 235 illus. c. 1977. Covers single exhaust models through 1976.

Haynes CZ Owner's Workshop Manual. softbound 27.3 x 21 cm (10-3/4 x 8¼") 93p, 244 illus. c. 1977. Covers 125, 175 and 175 Trail; 123 and 171cc 1969 to c. 1977.

DOUGLAS (British)

Carrick, Peter. Douglas. 88p, 137 illus. c. 1986. History of this make.

DUCATI (Italian)

Cathcart, Alan. Ducati Motorcycles. hardbound 7½ x 9½" 224p, 237 illus. 1983. From bicycle power to the racing machines.

Clymer Ducati Service, Repair Handbook. softbound 17.8 x 25.4 cm (7 x 10") 130p, 211 illus. Los Angeles: Clymer, c. 1977. Covers 160, 250, 350 and 450cc through 1974.

Ducati Singles. hardbound 7½ x 8½" 160p, 192 illus. Osprey Collector's Library, c. 1986. Covers all two-and four-stroke single cylinder motorcycles 1947-1974, plus Motrans.

Ducati Singles. softbound 17.8 x 25.4 cm (7 x 10") 130p, 211 illus. Los Angeles: Clymer, c. 1986. 160, 250, 350 and 450cc through 1974.

Ducati Workshop Manual. 144p, 139 illus. c. 1986. Covers overhead cam models 160, 250, 350 and 450.

Ducati Handbook and Workshop Manuals. 128p, 18 photographs. Covers 4- and 5-speed single overhead camshaft motorcycles.

Ducati 160/250/350 OHC Workshop Manual 1964-66. c. 1968.

Ducati Mk. III and Desmo Singles. softbound 27.3 x 21 cm (10-3/4 x 8¼") 116p. Haynes, c. 1986. Covers wide crankcase models, 239, 248, 340 and 435cc, 1969-1976.

Ducati V-Twins, 1971-77. softbound 27.3 x 21 cm (10-3/4 x 8¼") 148p. Haynes, c. 1986. Covers 748 and 846cc, ohc and Desmo, 1971-1977.

Walker, Mick. Ducati Twins. hardbound 7¼ x 8½" 192p, 160 illus. Osprey Collector's Library. 1985. Covers all bevel and belt drive V-twins and parallel twins from 1970 to c. 1985; 750, 860, 900, 1000 and smaller Pantah 350, 500, 650 and 750 versions.

EXCELSIOR (American)

Excelsior Motorcycle Sales Catalog. 12p, 26 illus. Reprint, c. 1986. Covers 61 cu. in. V-Twin (1920's).

FRANCIS-BARNETT (British)

Goddard, J.H. Francis-Barnett Maintenance and Repair Manual 1946-61. c. 1969.

Maintenance and Repair Manual. Pearson, c. 1968. All models, 1946-60.

HARLEY-DAVIDSON (American)

Arman, Mike and Kurt Heinrichs. Special Tools for Harley-Davidson. 63p, 61 illus. c. 1986. Covers all tools for V-Twins. Companion book to What Fits What.

Arman, Mike and Kurt Heinrichs. What Fits What on Harley-Davidson 1936-1981. 80p, 50 illus. c. 1986. Covers all V-twins from 1936.

Best Bikes: Special Issue No. 1. 160p, 271 photographs. c. 1986. Harley-Davidsons.

Chilton's Harley-Davidson V-Twins Repair and Tune-up Guide. softbound 17.8 x 26.1 cm (7 x 10¼") 212p, 221 illus. c. 1977. Covers Sportster 900 and 1000 Electra-Glide, Super Glide models 1965-1974.

Clymer Harley-Davidson Service, Repair Handbook. softbound 17.8 x 25.4 (7 x 10") 175p, 215 illus. Los Angeles: Clymer, c. 1977. Covers Sportster series 1959-1977.

_____. softbound 17.8 x 25.4 cm (7 x 10") 204p, 256 illus. Los Angeles: Clymer, c. 1977. Covers all 74 cubic-inch models 1959-76.

_____. softbound 17.8 x 25.4 cm (7 x 10") 309p, 559 illus. Los Angeles: Clymer, c. 1986. 74 and 80 cubic-inch V-Twins.

_____. softbound 17.8 x 25.4 cm (7 x 10") 280p, 507 illus. Los Angeles: Clymer, c. 1986. Harley-Davidson Sportsters, 1959-1984.

Easyriders: Motorcycles through the Years. 224p, 512 illus. c. 1986. From the first fifty years of Harley-Davidson.

Easy Rider. 1969. Video tape with Peter Fonda. 94 minutes. VHS and Beta.

Foster, Gerald. The Cult of the Harley-Davidson. softbound 8 x 9" 128p, 120 illus. c. 1986. Color photograph album.

_____. Harley-Davidson: The Cult Lives On. softbound 8 x 9" 50p, 85 illus. c. 1986. Color photograph album.

Harley-Davidson and Indian Maintenance and Repair Manual. Bagnall, c. 1969.

Harley-Davidson and Indian Maintenance Manual 1920-70. Bagnall, c. 1970.

Harley 61 Twin Model Owner's Manual. 4¼ x 9½" 20p, 16 illus. c. 1986.

Harley References in Chronological Order:

1912-1929 Harley All Models Service Bulletins, Vol. 1. 168p, 60 illus.

1915-1928 Harley Big Twins Owner's Manual Supplement. To be used with 1927-28 or 1929 Big Twins owner's manual. 4½ x 6½" 27p, 17 illus.

1916 Harley Motorcycle Catalog. 24p, 20 illus. Reprint of original sales catalog, c. 1986.

1917 Harley Sales Catalog. 6¼ x 10" 30p, 26 illus.

1922-26 Harley Parts Catalog. 6 x 9½" 76p.

1926-35 Harley Parts Catalog. 6¼ x 9¼" 192p.

1927-28 Harley Big Twins Owner's Manual. 4½ x 7" 34p, 28 illus. c. 1928.

1929 Harley 45 Twin and Single Owner's Manual. 4½ x 7" 44p, 31 illus.

1929 Harley 61 and 74 Twin Owner's Manual. 36p, 24 illus.

1930-36 Harley SV Big Twins Owner's Manual. 40p, 26 illus.

1930-39 Harley 45 SV Owner's Manual. 4½ x 6-3/4" 38p, 24 illus.

1930-40 Harley Shop Manual. 168p, 49 illus. Service bulletins from 1934 to 1939; special section on the 1936-40 61 OHV, and motor fitting spec chart on the 1925-29 big twins. Includes cylinder models.

1936 Harley 74 and 80 Twins Owner's Manual. 4¼ x 9½" 20p, 14 illus.

1936-48 Harley Big Twin Parts Catalog. 8½ x 11" 148p.

1937-47 Harley 45 SV and Servi-Car Owner's Manual. 4 x 9¼" 21p, 14 illus.

1940-47 Harley Big Twins Service Manual. 165p, 157 illus. Includes 30-39 SV big twins.

1940-50 Harley 45 SV and Servi-Car Parts Catalog. 124p, 76 illus.

1940-52 Harley 45 XV and Servi-Car Shop Manual. 80p, 70 illus.

1941 Harley Accessory Catalog. 72p, 340 illus. All accessories for 1937-48 OHV and SV models. Also clothing, tools, police equipment and paint colors.

1941 Harley 42WLA Military Owner's Manual. 76p, 46 illus.

1941-56 Harley Shop Manual. 160p, 200 photographs. Service bulletins 1941-1957 covering 1941-57 Knucklehead, Panhead, all Flatheads and overhaul on K-models. Includes Servicar and (20p) Model 125 and 165.

1947 Harley Sales Catalog. $7\frac{1}{2}$ x $5\frac{1}{2}$" 10p, 20 illus.

1948-54 Harley OHV Twin Owner's Manual. 4-3/4 x 6-3/4" 54p, 22 illus.

1948-57 Harley 45 SV and Servi-Car Owner's Manual. 4 x $9\frac{1}{4}$" 21p, 14 illus.

1949-57 Harley Twin Parts Catalog. $8\frac{1}{2}$ x 11" 156p.

1952-56 Harley K Model Owner's Manual. $5\frac{1}{2}$ x $8\frac{1}{2}$" 58p, 26 illus.

1955-57 Harley OHV Twins Owner's Manual. $5\frac{1}{2}$ x $8\frac{1}{2}$" 68p, 22 illus.

1957-69 Harley Service Bulletin, Vol. IV. 160p, 116 illus. All models.

1958-61 Harley OHV Twins Owner's Manual. $5\frac{1}{2}$ x $8\frac{1}{2}$" 60p, 24 illus.

1958-68 Harley Big Twin Parts Catalog. 149p.

1959-69 Harley-Davidson Electra Glide/Duo-Glide Service Manual. 232p, 358 illus.

1983 Antique Harley Cycle Supply Catalog. softbound $8\frac{1}{2}$ x 11" 160p, drawings. c. 1984. A catalog of parts, manuals and literature for older machines.

Harley-Davidson Electra Glide and Super Glide 1970-83. softbound 27.3 x 21 cm (10-3/4 x $8\frac{1}{4}$") 151p. c. 1986. Covers FL, FLH, FX and FXE models. 74 cubic inches from 1974.

Haynes Harley-Davidson Sportsters Owner's Workshop Manual. softbound 27.3 x 21 cm (10-3/4 x $8\frac{1}{4}$") 125p, 315 illus. c. 1977. Covers XL and XLCH models from 1970. Also issued in 164p, 380 illus 1970-83, published c. 1986.

Kolb, Hazel and Bill Stermer. On the Perimeter. 6¼ x 9" 227p. Travel, touring on a Harley-Davidson.

McClanahan, Carl. V-Twin Thunder. softbound 8½ x 11" 50p, 85 illus. Performance manual.

Sucher, Harry V. Harley-Davidson: The Milwaukee Marvel. hardbound 7 x 10" 283p, 201 illus. c. 1986. Includes the Excelsior motorcycle.

Tech Tips and Tricks. softbound 8 x 11" 128p, 216 illus. c. 1986. Edited by staff of Easyriders magazine.

Unofficial Flat Rate Manual for Harley-Davidson Motorcycles. unbound, 24p.

van Drie, Hans and Gerard vd Akker. Harley-Davidson in Nederland. 96p, 204 illus. In Dutch and English.

Wright, David. The Harley-Davidson Motor Company: An Official Eighty-Year History. hardbound 7¼ x 9-3/4" 280p, 250 illus, 14 in color. c. 1986.

Yesterdaze: People and Bikes in the Wind Years Gone By. 170p, 344 photographs. c. 1986. Includes several Indian motorcycles.

HENDERSON (American)

1918 Henderson Sales Catalog. 7½ x 10" 16p, 20 illus. c. 1986.

1928 Henderson Super X Sales Catalog. 12p, 20 illus. c. 1986.

HODAKA (Japanese)

Chilton Hodaka Repair and Tune-up Guide. softbound 17.8 x 26.1 cm (7 x 10¼") 132p, 160 illus. c. 1977. Covers Ace 90, 100, 100B, 100MX, Wombat and Combat Wombat models from 1964 to 1973.

Clymer Hodaka Service, Repair Handbook. softbound 17.8 x 25.4 cm (7 x 10") 161p, 180 illus. Los Angeles: Clymer, c. 1977. Covers 90-125cc singles, 1964 to 1975.

HONDA (Japanese)

Bacon, Roy. Honda: The Early Classic Motorcycles. hardbound 7½ x 8½" 192p, 160 illus. Osprey Collector's Library, 1986. Covers 1946 to the 1977 Goldwing, every production single,

112 / Motorcycle Books

twin, four, and racing Honda. Includes CB72, CB77, 450 Black Bomber, KO 750, CR110, and CR93.

Carrick, Peter. The Story of Honda Motor Cycles. hardbound 136p, 90 illus. c. 1977. Covers 1948 to c. 1977.

Chilton's Honda XL Series and Tune-up Guide. softbound 17.8 x 26.1 cm (7 x 10¼") 169p, 310 illus. c. 1977. Covers 350, 250, 175, 125, 100 and 70cc models from 1972 to 1975.

Childton's Honda Fours Repair and Tune-up Guide. softbound 17.8 x 26.1 cm (7 x 10¼") 165p, 400 illus. second edition, c. 1977. Covers all four-cylinder models through 1974.

Chilton's Honda 450/500 Twins Repair and Tune-up Guide. softbound 17.8 x 26.1 cm (7 x 10¼") 165p, 300 illus. c. 1977. Covers all 450/500 Twins, 1966 to 1976.

Chilton's Honda 350/360 Twins Repair and Tune-up Guide. softbound 17.8 x 26.1 cm (7 x 10¼") 170p, 340 illus. c. 1977. Covers all 350/360 Twins, 1968 to 1975.

Chilton's Honda 125-200 Twins Repair and Tune-up Guide. softbound 17.8 x 26.1 cm (7 x 10¼") 153p, 300 illus. c. 1977. Covers all 125-200 Twins, 1969 to 1976.

Chilton's Honda Twins Repair and Tune-up Guide. softbound 17.8 x 26.1 cm (7 x 10¼") 148p, 275 illus. c. 1977. Covers 5-speed and popular 4-speed models 1966 to 1972.

Chilton's Honda Singles Repair and Tune-up Guide. softbound 17.8 x 26.1 cm (7 x 10¼") 198p, 330 illus. second edition, c. 1977.

Chilton's Honda Elsinores Repair and Tune-up Guide. softbound 17.8 x 26.1 cm (7 x 10¼") 145p, 300 illus. c. 1977. Covers CR and MT models through 1975.

Clymer Honda Service, Repair Handbook. softbound 17.8 x 25.4 (7 x 10") 228p, 460 illus. Los Angeles: Clymer, c. 1977. Covers 100-350cc 4-stroke singles, 1970 to 1977.

_____. softbound 17.8 x 25.4 cm (7 x 10") 144p, 225 illus. Los Angeles: Clymer, c. 1977. Covers 50-90cc singles, 1963 to 1976.

_____. softbound 17.8 x 25.4 cm (7 x 10") 151p, 230 illus. Los Angeles: Clymer, c. 1977. Covers 125-250cc Elsinores, 1973 to 1977.

_____. softbound 17.8 x 25.4 cm (7 x 10") 161p, 255 illus. c. 1977. Los Angeles: Clymer, c. 1977. Covers 125-360cc Twins, 1964 to 1976.

_____. softbound 17.8 x 25.4 cm (7 x 10") 176p, 392 illus. Los Angeles: Clymer, c. 1977. Covers 250-305cc Twins. All years to c. 1977.

_____. softbound 17.8 x 25.4 cm (7 x 10") 184p, 310 illus. Los Angeles: Clymer, c. 1977. Covers 450 and 500cc Twins, 1965 to 1976.

_____. softbound 17.8 x 25.4 cm (7 x 10") 225p, 380 illus. Los Angeles: Clymer, c. 1977. Covers 350-550cc Fours, 1972 to 1977.

_____. softbound 17.8 x 25.4 cm (7 x 10") 224p, 445 illus. Los Angeles: Clymer, c. 1977. Covers 750cc Fours, 1969 to 1977.

_____. softbound 17.8 x 25.4 cm (7 x 10") 169p, 345 illus. Los Angeles: Clymer, c. 1977. Covers GL-1000, 1975 to 1976.

_____. Honda Singles. softbound 17.8 x 25.4 cm (7 x 10") 351p, 635 illus. Los Angeles: Clymer, c. 1986. Covers 50-90cc, 1965 to 1983.

_____. Honda ATC250R Singles 1981-84. softbound 17.8 x 25.4 cm (7 x 10") 233p, 519 illus. Los Angeles: Clymer, c. 1986.

_____. Honda XR75 and XR80 Singles. softbound 17.8 x 25.4 cm (7 x 10") 224p, 405 illus. Los Angeles: Clymer, c. 1986. Covers 1975 to 1984.

_____. Honda Odyssey. softbound 17.8 x 25.4 cm (7 x 10") 234p, 424 illus. Los Angeles: Clymer, c. 1986. Covers 1977 to 1984.

_____. Honda 4-Stroke Singles. softbound 17.8 x 25.4 cm (7 x 10") 352p, 637 illus. Los Angeles: Clymer, c. 1986. Covers 100-350cc, 1969 to 1982.

_____. Honda Elsinore Singles. softbound 17.8 x 25.4 cm (7 x 10") 149p, 222 illus. Los Angeles: Clymer, c. 1986. Covers 125 and 250cc, 1973 to 1980.

_____. Honda XL/XR125-200 Singles. softbound 17.8 x 25.4 cm (7 x 10"). Los Angeles: Clymer, c. 1986. Covers 1979 to 1983.

_____. Honda XR250/500 and XL250/500S Singles. softbound 17.8 x 25.4 cm (7 x 10") 345p, 624 illus. Los Angeles: Clymer, c. 1986. Covers 1978 to 1983.

_____. Honda ATC70-110 Singles. softbound 17.8 x 25.4 cm (7 x 10") 271p, 491 illus. Los Angeles: Clymer, c. 1986. Covers 1970 to 1984.

_____. Honda ATC185 and 200 Singles. softbound 17.8 x 25.4 cm (7 x 10") 375p, 679 illus. Los Angeles: Clymer, c. 1986. Covers 1980 to 1984.

_____. Honda Twins. softbound 17.8 x 25.4 cm (7 x 10") 126p, 372 illus. Los Angeles: Clymer, c. 1986. Covers 125-200cc, 1964 to 1977.

_____. Honda Twinstar. softbound 17.8 x 25.4 cm (7 x 10") 237p, 623 illus. Los Angeles: Clymer, c. 1986. Covers 1978 to 1981.

_____. Honda Twins. softbound 17.8 x 25.4 cm (7 x 10") 171p, 450 illus. Los Angeles: Clymer, c. 1986. Covers 250 and 350cc, 1964 to 1974.

_____. Honda Twins. softbound 17.8 x 25.4 cm (7 x 10") 132p, 395 illus. Los Angeles: Clymer, c. 1986. Covers 250 and 360cc, 1974 to 1977.

_____. Honda 250 and 450cc Twins. softbound 17.8 x 25.4 cm (7 x 10") 288p, 521 illus. Los Angeles: Clymer, c. 1986. Covers 1978 to 1983.

_____. Honda Scrambler Twins. softbound 17.8 x 25.4 cm (7 x 10") 176p, 392 illus. Los Angeles: Clymer, c. 1986. Covers 250-305cc, all years to c. 1986.

_____. Honda Twins. softbound 17.8 x 25.4 cm (7 x 10") 179p, 306 illus. Los Angeles: Clymer, c. 1986. Covers 450 and 500cc, 1965 to 1977.

_____. Honda CX500 Twins. softbound 17.8 x 25.4 cm (7 x 10") 296p, 536 illus. Los Angeles: Clymer, c. 1986. Covers 1978 to 1983.

_____. Honda Fours. softbound 17.8 x 25.4 cm (7 x 10") 195p, 377 illus. Los Angeles: Clymer, c. 1986. Covers 350-550cc, 1972 to 1978.

_____. Honda CB650 Fours. softbound 17.8 x 25.4 cm (7 x 10") 327p, 872 illus. Los Angeles: Clymer, c. 1986. Covers 1979 to 1982.

_____. Honda CB750 SOHC Fours. softbound 17.8 x 25.4 cm (7 x 10") 216p, 475 illus. Los Angeles: Clymer, c. 1986. Covers 1969 to 1978.

_____. Honda CB750 DOHC Fours. softbound 17.8 x 25.4 cm (7 x 10") 308p, 778 illus. Los Angeles: Clymer, c. 1986. Covers 1979 to 1981.

_____. Honda CB 900 Fours. softbound 17.8 x 25.4 cm (7 x 10") 379p, 686 illus. Los Angeles: Clymer, c. 1986. Covers 1980 to 1983.

_____. Honda GL 1000 and 1100 Fours. softbound 17.8 x 25.4 cm (7 x 10") 302p, 547 illus. Los Angeles: Clymer, c. 1986. Covers 1975 to 1983.

_____. Clymer Honda V45 and V65 1982-1983. softbound 17.8 x 25.4 cm (7 x 10") 309p, 559 illus. Los Angeles: Clymer, c. 1986.

Glenn, Harold T. Glenn's Honda. 218p. New York: c. 1971.

Haynes Honda 50 Owner's Workshop Manual. softbound 27.3 x 21 cm (10-3/4 x 8¼") 111p, 245 illus. c. 1977. Covers ohv, ohc, scooters and bikes, 1962 to c. 1977.

Haynes Honda 65, 70 and 90 Owner's Workshop Manual. softbound 27.3 x 21 cm (10-3/4 x 8¼") 94 p, 176 illus. c. 1977. Covers all models, ohv, ohc, 1964 to c. 1977.

Haynes Honda CB100, CB125X and SL125 Owner's Workshop Manual. softbound 27.3 x 21 cm (10-3/4 x 8¼") 93p, 197 illus. c. 1977. Covers 99cc, and 122cc, 1970 to c. 1977.

Haynes Honda 125, 160, 175 and 200 Twins Owner's Workshop Manual. softbound 27.3 x 21 cm (10-3/4 x 8¼") 118p, 255 illus. c. 1977. Covers 122, 161, 174, 198cc 1964 to c. 1977.

Haynes Honda 125 and 175 Elsinore Owner's Workshop Manual. softbound 27.3 x 21 cm (10-3/4 x 8¼") 116p, 266 illus. c. 1977. Covers 123 and 171cc, 1973 to c. 1977.

Haynes Honda 250 Elsinore Owner's Workshop Manual. softbound 27.3 x 21 cm (10-3/4 x 8¼") 95p, 225 illus. c. 1977. Covers 248cc, 1973 to c. 1977.

Haynes Honda 250 and 350 Twins Owner's Workshop Manual. softbound 27.3 x 21 cm (10-3/4 x 8¼") 112p, 215 illus. c. 1977. Covers 249 and 325cc, 1968 to c. 1977.

Haynes Honda XL250 and 350 Trail Bikes Owner's Workshop Manual. softbound 27.3 x 21 cm (10-3/4 x 8¼") 117p, 315 illus. c. 1977. Covers 248 and 348cc OHC, 1972 to c. 1977.

Haynes Honda 4, 500 and 350 Owner's Workshop Manual. softbound 27.3 x 21 cm (10-3/4 x 8¼") 107p, 200 illus. c. 1977. Covers all models, 4 cyl. 498cc and 437cc, 1971 to c. 1977.

Haynes Honda CB 450 Twins Owner's Workshop Manual. softbound 27.3 x 21 cm (10-3/4 x 8¼") 105p, 210 illus. c. 1977. Covers 444cc, 4- and 5-speed models, 1965 to c. 1977.

116 / Motorcycle Books

Haynes Honda 750 Four Owner's Workshop Manual. softbound 27.3 x 21 cm (10-3/4 x 8¼") 128p, 280 illus. c. 1977. Covers 4-cylinder 736cc, all models 1969 to c. 1977.

Haynes Honda XR 75 Dirt Bikes Owner's Workshop Manual. softbound 27.3 x 21 cm (10-3/4 x 8¼") 88p, 225 illus. c. 1977. Covers 72cc, all models, 1972 to c. 1977.

Haynes Honda 400 and 550 Fours Owner's Workshop Manual. softbound 27.3 x 21 cm (10-3/4 x 8¼") 126p, 270 illus. c. 1977. Covers 408 and 544cc, 1973 to c. 1977.

Haynes Honda 250 G5 and 360 Twins Owner's Workshop Manual. softbound 27.3 x 21 cm (10-3/4 x 8¼") 88p, 223 illus. c. 1977. Covers 249 and 356cc, 1974 to c. 1977.

Haynes Honda GL 1000 Gold Wing Owner's Workshop Manual. softbound 27.3 x 21 cm (10-3/4 x 8¼") 157p, 402 illus. c. 1977. Covers 4-cylinder 999cc, 1975 to c. 1977.

Honda Maintenance and Repair Manual. Pearson, c. 1968. Covers 1960 to 1967.

Honda 50/125/250 Handbook 1961-66. Pitman, c. 1968. Also: 125/150 for years 1960-65.

Honda Shop Manuals and Handbooks. 8½ x 11", 210p. Los Angeles: Clymer. Covers 50cc models.

_____. 8½ x 11" 176p. Los Angeles: Clymer. Covers 125 and 150cc models.

_____. 8¼ x 11" 192p. Los Angeles: Clymer. Covers 250 and 300cc models, 1960-67.

Honda Workshop Manual. c. 1968. Covers 50 C100/C1100, 1963-67.

Honda Handbook. 90cc, 1964-66. Pitman, c. 1968.

Honda Workshop Manual. 125/150 C92/C95, 1961-67. c. 1968.

_____. 250/300 C72/C77, 1961-67. c. 1968.

Honda All Models Maintenance and Repair Manual, 1960-67. Pearson, c. 1969.

Honda Twins Handbook, 1961-68. Pitman, c. 1969.

Rae, Peter. Honda Gold Wing. softbound 7-3/4 x 10½" 135p, 100 illus, 12 in color. c. 1986. History of this model.

Myers, Chris. Honda. 64p, 36 color photographs. c. 1986.

Sakiya, Tetsuo. Honda Motor: The Men, the Management, the Machines. 242p, 52 illus. c. 1986.

Sanders, Sol. Honda: The Man and His Machines. 207p, 20 photographs. c. 1977. First biography of Soichiro Honda.

Shoemark, Pete. Honda CB 750 Super Profile. 56p, 92 illus, 20 in color. c. 1986.

Thorpe, John. Book of the Honda Service Manual. 57 charts, drawings and wiring diagrams. Covers all models up to 1964, inclusive.

_____. Book of the Honda 90, 1964-66.

Video. Honda: The Technology. 35 minutes on VHS and Beta. Tests and demonstrations to late 1982.

Woollett, Mick. Honda. hardbound 8½ x 11½" 160p, 210 illus, 27 in color. c. 1986. History of the factory from 1948 to 1983.

HRD (British)

See: Vincent. H.R. Davies motorcycles production was bought by Vincent.

HUSQVARNA (Swedish)

Clymer Husqvarna Service, Repair Handbook. Husqvarna Singles. softbound 17.8 x 25.4 cm (7 x 10") 163p, 285 illus. Los Angels: Clymer, c. 1977.

Haynes Husqvarna Competition Models Owner's Workshop Manual. softbound 27.3 x 21 cm (10-3/4 x 8¼") 94p, 180 illus. c. 1977. Covers all capacities, 1972 to c. 1977.

INDIAN (American)

Harley-Davidson and Indian Maintenance and Repair Manual. Bagnall, c. 1969.

Indian Motorcycle Model 340-B and 344 Operation and Maintenance. 128p, 184 illus. c. 1986.

Indian References in Chronological Order:

Indian Motorcycles 1912. 24p, 30 illus. Bagnall Publishing Co. reprinted, c. 1986.

1903 Indian Sales Catalog. 12p, 5 illus.

1920 Indian Scout Type G-20 Owner's Manual. 5-3/4 x 8-3/4" 16p, 8 illus.

1928 Indian Sales Catalog. 9½ x 6" 20p, 26 illus.

1932 Indian Scout, 74, 4 Cylinder Owner's Manual. 40p, 27 illus.

1933-1942 Indian 4 Overhaul Manual. 29p.

1936-1953 Indian 74 Shop Manual. 54p, 62 illus.

1940-1953 Indian Owner's Manual. 5 x 7" 42p, 29 illus.

1942 Indian 741-B Military Owner's Manual. 120p, 102 illus.

Sucher, Harry. The Iron Redskin. hardbound 335p, 220 illus. c. 1977. History of the factory, Springfield, Massachusetts.

JAP (British)

Clew, Jeff. J.A.P.: The Vintage Years. 255p, 138 illus. c. 1986. Covers John A. Prestwich, builder of 1920 and 30's engines.

Haycraft. J.A.P. Engines. Models 1927-52.

JAP Handbook 1927-52. Pitman, c. 1968. Includes AJW/Cotton.

KAWASAKI (Japanese)

Bacon, Roy. Kawasaki: Sunrise to Z1. hardbound 7½ x 8½" 192p, 165 illus. Osprey Collector's Library, c. 1984. Covers all singles, twins, triples and 900 fours, 1962 to 1976.

Chilton Kawasaki Singles Repair and Tune-up Guide. softbound 17.8 x 26.1 cm (7 x 10¼") 165p, 325 illus. c. 1977. Covers single-cylinder two-stroke models 1969-75.

Chilton's Kawasaki Triples Repair and Tune-up Guide. softbound 17.8 x 26.1 cm (7 x 10¼") 149p, 320 illus. c. 1977. Covers all models, 1969-75.

Chilton's Kawasaki 900Z1 Repair and Tune-up Guide. softbound 17.8 x 26.1 cm (7 x 10¼") 180p, 500 illus. c. 1977. Covers 1973-74.

Clymer Kawasaki Service, Repair Handbook. softbound 17.8 x 25.4 cm (7 x 10") 212p, 385 illus. c. 1977. Covers 80-450cc singles, 1966-77.

_____. softbound 17.8 x 25.4 cm (7 x 10") 132p, 260 illus. c. 1977. Covers 250 and 350cc Twins, 1966-77.

_____. softbound 17.8 x 25.4 cm (7 x 10") 135p, 220 illus. c. 1977. Covers KZ400, 1974-77.

_____. softbound 17.8 x 25.4 cm (7 x 10") 169p, 385 illus. c. 1977. Covers 250-750 Triples, 1969-76.

_____. softbound 17.8 x 25.4 cm (7 x 10") 238p, 485 illus. c. 1977. Covers 900 and 1000cc Fours, 1973-77.

_____. Kawasaki 80-350cc Rotary Valve Singles. softbound 17.8 x 25.4 cm (7 x 10") 217p, 385 illus. Los Angeles: Clymer, c. 1986. Covers 1966-80.

_____. Kawasaki KDX80-420 Singles. softbound 17.8 x 25.4 cm (7 x 10") 187p, 463 illus. Los Angeles: Clymer, c. 1986. Covers 1979-1981.

_____. Kawasaki KX80-450 Piston-port Singles. softbound 17.8 x 25.4 cm (7 x 10"). Los Angeles: Clymer, c. 1986. Covers 1974-1981.

_____. Kawasaki KZ200 and KZ250. softbound 17.8 x 25.4 cm (7 x 10") 219p, 547 illus. Los Angeles: Clymer, c. 1986. Covers 1978-1983.

_____. Kawasaki A-Series Twins. softbound 17.8 x 25.4 cm (7 x 10") 132p, 260 illus. Los Angeles: Clymer, c. 1986. Covers 250 and 350cc, all years to 1986.

_____. Kawasaki KZ400 and KZ440 Twins. softbound 17.8 x 25.4 cm (7 x 10") 244p, 442 illus. Los Angeles: Clymer, c. 1986. Covers 1974-1983.

_____. Kawasaki KZ500 and 550 Fours. softbound 17.8 x 25.4 cm (7 x 10"). Los Angeles: Clymer, c. 1986. Covers 1979-1984.

_____. Kawasaki KZ650 Fours. softbound 17.8 x 25.4 cm (7 x 10") 318p, 576 illus. Los Angeles: Clymer, c. 1986. Covers 1977-1983.

_____. Kawasaki KZ750 Fours. softbound 17.8 x 25.4 cm (7 x 10") 319p, 577 illus. Los Angeles: Clymer, c. 1986. Covers 1980-1983.

_____. Kawasaki 900/1000cc Fours 1973-80. softbound 17.8 x 25.4 cm (7 x 10") 358p, 785 illus. Los Angeles: Clymer, c. 1986.

MAICO (German)

Clymer Maico Service, Repair Handbook. softbound 17.8 x 25.4 cm (7 x 10") 112p, 282 illus. Los Angeles: Clymer, c. 1977. Covers 250-501cc singles, 1968-1975.

Haynes Maico Competition Models Owner's Workshop Manual. softbound 27.3 x 21 cm (10-3/4 x 8¼") 95p, 275 illus. c. 1977. Covers 124, 247, 386, 438 and 501cc.

MATCHLESS (British)

AJS and Matchless Single and Twin Spares List. 56p, 30 illus. c. 1986. Covers the 1956, 350cc 16MS, 16 MCT, 16 MCS 500cc 18S, 18CS and 1958 16MS, 16CT, 16CS, 500cc 18S, 18CS, 20 600cc 30, 30CS.

AJS and Matchless Single Motorcycles 1957-66 Shop Manual. 125p, 38 illus. c. 1986. Covers 1958-1964 Lightweight 250cc and 350cc models G2, G2S, G2CS, G2CSR, 14, 14S, 14CS, 14CSR, G5, 8 and 1957 to 1966 heavyweight 350cc, 500cc and 600cc models G3, G3S, GsLS, G3LCS, G80, G80S, G80CS, TCS, 16, 16S, 16C, 16MC, 16MCS, 18, 18S and 18CS.

Bacon, Roy. AJS and Matchless: The Postwar Models. 192p, 165 illus. Osprey Collector's Library, 1983. Covers lightweight singles and twins from 1945.

Haycraft. Matchless Singles. Models 1955-66.

Hide, Reg. Matchless 30 and 500cc Heavyweight Singles 1939-1955. Maintenance Manual. 59p, 65 illus. Temple Press, c. 1969.

Jackson, Keigh and Deryk Wylde. Matchless G3L and G80 Super Profile. 56p, 90 illus, 20 in color. c. 1986. Detailed profile with pictorial evolution.

Main-Smith, Bruce. The First AMC Racing Scene. softbound 64p, 126 photographs. c. 1986. Photographic history of postwar Matchless and AJS racing machines.

Neill, F.W. AJS and Matchless Twin. Models 1955-65.

_____. Matchless Singles Maintenance and Repair Manual 1945-60. c. 1969.

In chronological order:

Matchless Maintenance and Repair Manual. Pearson, c. 1968. Covers 350 and 500cc Singles 1945-60.

Matchless Motorcycles 1939-55. Published by Motor Cycling (Magazine), c. 1969.

Matchless 350 and 500 Singles handbook 1945-60. Pitman, c. 1968.

Matchless and 1965-66 Norton 350/500 singles handbook 1955-66. c. 1970.

Matchless 350/500 singles handbook 1955-66. Pitman, c. 1970.

Matchless Twins Workshop Manual 1955-1966. Lodgemark, c. 1970.

MONTESA (Spanish)

Clymer Montesa Service, Repair Handbook. softbound 17.8 x 25.4 cm (7 x 19") 129p, 220 illus. Los Angeles: Clymer, c. 1977. Covers 123-360cc singles 1965-75.

MOTO GUZZI (Italian)

Chilton's Moto Guzzi Repair and Tune-up Guide. softbound 17.8 x 26.1 cm (7 x 10¼") 163p, 220 illus. c. 1977. Covers all V7, V750 Ambassador and Dorado models from 1966-1972.

Colombo, Mario. Moto Guzzi: Genius and Sport. 127p, 96 illus. c. 1986. Text in English and Italian.

MV AUGUSTA
see under
AUGUSTA

MX (German)

Haynes MX 150 and 250 Owner's Workshop Manual. softbound 27.3 x 21 cm (10-3/4 x 8¼") 103p, 287 illus. c. 1977. Covers 143, 243 cc 1969 to c. 1977.

NORMAN (British)

Nippy or Lido 1962-63. c. 1969.

NORTON (British)

Ayton, C.J. International Norton Super Profile. 56p, 87 illus, 20 in color. c. 1986. History, evolution and specifications with photographs from first bikes to last production model.

_____. Manx Norton Super Profile. hardbound 8¼ x 11" 56p, 93 illus. 1985. History.

Bacon, Roy. Norton Singles. hardbound 7½ x 8½" 192p, 165 illus. Osprey Collector's Library, 1986. Foreword by Geoff Duke. Covers Manx, Inter and all overhead valve singles from 1927 to 1966.

_____. The Norton Twins. hardbound 7½ x 8½" 191p, 167 illus. Osprey Collector's Library, c. 1986. Covers all postwar 500, 600, 650, 750, 850 and lightweight twins, as well as Wulf, Wankel, Cosworth and AMC Nortons.

Chilton's Norton 750 and 850 Repair and Tune-up Guide. softbound 17.8 x 26.1 cm (7 x 10¼") 165p, 220 illus. Covers all Commando, Atlas, G15CS, N15CS and P-11 models from 1966 to 1972.

Clew, Jeff. Norton Commando Super Profile. 56p, 90 illus, 20 in color. c. 1986. History, with documentary photographs.

Clymer Norton Service, Repair Handbook. softbound 17.8 x 25.4 cm (7 x 10") 207p, 45p illus. Los Angeles: Clymer, c. 1977. Covers 750 and 850cc, all years to c. 1977.

Dunstall, Paul. Norton Tuning. 32p, 72 illus. c. 1986. Covers all bikes using the 647 and 745cc engines.

The First Knocker Norton Scene. softbound 64p, 132 illus. c. 1986. All years SOCH and DOCH.

Garratt. Norton Maintenance and Repair Manual 1948-62. c. 1969.

Haycraft. Norton. Models 1955-62.

_____. Norton Dominator Twins. Models 1955-65.

Haynes Norton Commando Owner's Workshop Manual. softbound 27.3 x 21 cm (10-3/4 x 8¼") 141p, 237 illus. c. 1977. Covers 745 and 828cc models from 1967 to c. 1977.

Haynes Norton Twins Workshop Manual. softbound 27.3 x 21 cm (10-3/4 x 8¼") 132p, 239 illus. c. 1977. Covers 88, 88SS, 99, 99SS, 650, 650SS, Atlas, Mercury, 497cc, 597cc, 657cc and 745cc, 1957 to 1970.

Holliday, Bob. The Norton Story. hardbound 128p, 92 illus. c. 1977. 1900 to 1976.

_____. The Unapproachable Norton. hardbound 7 x 9" 104p, 193 illus. c. 1986.

Main-Smith, Bruce (publisher). Norton Motorcycles 1928-55. 62p, 38 illus. Motor Cycling (Magazine), c. 1969. Also: Temple Press. 348 to 596cc. Norton numbering system 1923 to 1963.

Matchless and 1965-66 Norton 350/500 Singles Handbook 1955-66. c. 1970.

Neill, F. Norton Service and Overhaul Manual. 176p, 123 illus. c. 1986. Covers the single cylinder 348cc 50 and 490cc ES2, and the twin cylinder 250cc Jubilee, 350cc Navigator, 400cc Electra, 497cc 88, 88 deluxe, 88SS, 99 Standard, 99SS, 99 deluxe, 650 standard, 650 deluxe, 650 America, 650SS, 650 Manxman, 750 Atlas, 750 Scrambler, and 750 G15CS.

Norton Dominator Owner's Manual. 40p, 18 illus. c. 1986.

Norton 88 and 99 Owner's Manual. 38p, 25 illus. c. 1986.

1928 Norton Owner's Manual. 39p, 23 illus. c. 1986.

1934 Norton Owner's Manual. 47p, 18 illus. c. 1986.

1938 Norton Owner's Manual. 5½ x 8½" 51p, 17 illus. c. 1986.

1938 Norton Owner's Manual. 33 p. c. 1986.

Norton Maintenance Manual 1939-55. c. 1969.

Norton Singles Handbook, 1955-62. Pitman, c. 1969.

Norton Singles 1955-62 Handbook. Pitman, c. 1968.

Norton Dominator Twins Handbook 1955-65. Pitman, c. 1968.

Norton Models 50 and ES2fHandbook, 1965-66. Pitman, c. 1969.

Norton Twins All Models Workshop Manual 1960-67. c. 1968.

Norton Lightweight Twins and Heavyweight Twins 1959-1968. Los Angeles: Clymer and Norton, c. 1969. Jubilee, Navigator, Electra and 88, 99, 650SS, 750 Atlas and 750G15CS.

NSU(German)

NSU Handbook Prima 1957-61. Pitman, c. 1968.

NSU Prima D 1956-62 Workshop Manual, c. 1968.

NSU Quickly 1953-67. Pitman, c. 1968. Also published as for the years 1953-65.

NSU Prima V, III, IIIK, IIIKL 1958-63 Workshop Manual. c. 1968.

OSSA (Spanish)

Clymer Ossa Service, Repair Handbook. 154p, 220 illus. c. 1977. Covers 125-250cc singles, 1971 to 1976.

PANTHER (British and German)

Jones, Barry M. The Story of Panther Motorcycles. 136p, 124 illus. c. 1986.

Panther 250 and 350 1932-58 Handbook. Pitman, c. 1968.

Panther 600 and 650 Models 100 and 120 1938-66 Handbook. Pitman, c. 1968.

PHILLIPS

Phillips 1962-63. c. 1969.

Phillips Gadabout Mark IV 1962-63 Workshop Manual. c. 1968.

PUCH (Austrian)

Haynes Maxi Mopeds Owner's Workshop Manual. softbound 27.3 x 21 cm (10-3/4 x 8¼") 87p, 150 illus. c. 1977. Covers all models from 1969 to c. 1977.

Puch Alpine RL125 and RLA 125 1957-69 Workshop Manual. c. 1968.

Puch 1957-68. c. 1969.

Puch 250 Motorcycles 1957-69. c. 1969.

RELIANT

Reliant Regal 1939-65 Handbook. Pitman, c. 1968.

ROYAL ENFIELD (British)

Bacon, Roy. Royal Enfield: The Postwar Models. hardbound 7½ x 8½" 160p, 150 photographs. Osprey Collector's Library, c. 1986. Covers 125, 150, 250, 350, 500, 700 and 750 singles and twins. History and specifications.

Booker. C.A.E. Royal Enfield Maintenance and Repair Manual 1937-60. c. 1969.

Hartley, Peter. The Story of Royal Enfield Motorcycles. 128p, 98 illus. c. 1986.

Haycraft. Royal Enfield. Models 1946-62. Four-stroke singles.

Royal Enfield 4-stroke Singles 1946-62. Pitman, c. 1968.

Royal Enfield 250 and 350 4-stroke Singles Handbook 1958-66. Pitman, c. 1968.

Royal Enfield 736cc Interceptor Workshop Manual 1963-67. c. 1968.

1937 Royal Enfield Owner's Manual. 32p, 8 illus. c. 1986.

1953 Royal Enfield Owner's Manual. 4-3/4 x 7" 51p, 21 illus. c. 1986.

RUDGE (British)

Hartley, Peter. The Story of Rudge Motorcycles. 128p, 101 illus. c. 1986.

Ransom, R.P. Rudge.

Reynolds, Bryan. Don't Trudge It--Rudge It. 174p, 110 illus. History to 1939.

Rudge Maintenance and Repair Manual. Pearson, c. 1968. All models 1934-39.

1939 Rudge Sales Catalog. 10 x 7-3/4" 11p, 12 illus. c. 1986.

SACHS (German)

Clymer Sachs Engine Service, Repair Handbook. softbound 7 x 10" 140p, 225 illus. Los Angeles: Clymer c. 1977. Covers 100 and 125cc, 1968-74.

SCOTT (British)

Clew, Jeff. The Scott Motorcycle: The Yowling Two-Stroke. hardbound 239p, 137 illus. c. 1977. History.

Main-Smith, Bruce. The First Scott Scene. 64p, 126 illus by Bruce Main-Smith. Pub. by Bruce Main-Smith, c. 1977.

Smith, Philip H. Scott Motorcycle Trials, 1914-37. c. 1969.

SUNBEAM (British)

BSA Sunbeam and Triumph Tigress Handbook 1959-65. Pitman, c. 1969.

Champ, Robert C. The Sunbeam Motorcycle. 205p, 157 illus. c. 1986.

Hide, Reg. Sunbeam Four-Stroke Singles 1928-39. softbound 68p, 80 illus. c. 1977.

Sunbeam All Models Handbook 1928-39. Pitman, c. 1968.

Sunbeam 500 Twins Handbook 1946-57. Putman, c. 1968.

SUZUKI (Japanese)

Aspel, Geoff. Suzuki. 64p, 36 color photographs. c. 1986. Concise history.

Bacon, Roy. Suzuki Two-Strokes. Osprey Collector's Library, c. 1986. All two-stroke singles, twins and triples plus RE5 from 1952 to 1979.

Battersby, Ray. Team Suzuki. hardbound $7\frac{1}{2}$ x 10" 240p, 250 illus. c. 1986. Analyses of factory road racing motorcycles, and history from 1953 to 1982.

Chilton's Suzuki Singles and Twins Repair and Tune-up Guide. softbound 17.8 x 26.1 cm (7 x $10\frac{1}{4}$") 127p, 250 illus. c. 1977. Covers 1970-74.

Chilton's Suzuki Triples Repair and Tune-up Guide. softbound 17.8 x 26.1 cm (7 x $10\frac{1}{4}$") 120p, 275 illus. c. 1977. Covers GT 380, GT 550, GT 750 models 1972-74.

Clymer Suzuki Service, Repair Handbook. softbound 17.8 x 25.4 cm (7 x 10") 131p, 317 illus. Los Angeles: Clymer, c. 1977. Covers 125-400cc singles, 1964-76.

_____. softbound 17.8 x 25.4 cm (7 x 10") 149p, 354 illus. Los Angeles: Clymer, c. 1977. Covers 125-500 cc twins, 1964-76.

_____. softbound 17.8 x 25.4 cm (7 x 10") 146p, 372 illus. Los Angeles: Clymer, c. 1977. Covers 50-120cc singles, 1964-77.

_____. softbound 17.8 x 25.4 cm (7 x 10") 159p, 262 illus. Los Angeles: Clymer, c. 1977. Covers 380-750cc, Triples, 1972-76.

Haynes Suzuki Student and B100P Owner's Workshop Manual. softbound 27.3 x 21 cm (10-3/4 x 8¼") 90p, 232 illus. c. 1977. Covers 118cc, 2-stroke, 1967 to c. 1977.

Haynes Suzuki GT 125 and 185 Twins Owner's Workshop Manual. softbound 27.3 x 21 cm (10-3/4 x 8¼") 97p, 260 illus. c. 1977. Covers 125, 183cc, 2-stroke 1973 to c. 1977.

Haynes Suzuki Trail Bikes Owner's Workshop Manual. softbound 27.3 x 21 cm (10-3/4 x 8¼") 152p, 362 illus. c. 1977. Covers 89, 97, 123, 246 and 396cc from 1971 to c. 1977.

Haynes Suzuki 250 and 350 Owner's Workshop Manual. softbound 27.3 x 21 cm (10-3/4 x 8¼") 112p, 285 illus. c. 1977. Covers all 250 and 350 twins, 247 and 315cc 1964 to c. 1977.

Haynes Suzuki GT 380 and GT 550 3-Cylinder Models Owner's Workshop Manual. softbound 18.8 x 25.4 cm (7 x 10") 110p, 278 illus. c. 1977. Covers 371 and 544cc, 2-stroke, 1972 to c. 1977.

Haynes Suzuki 500 Twin Owner's Workshop Manual. softbound 17.8 x 25.4 cm (7 x 10") 88p, 172 illus. c. 1977. Covers all models 492cc 1968 to c. 1977.

Haynes Suzuki 750, 3-Cylinder Models Owner's Workshop Manual. softbound 17.8 x 25.4 cm (7 x 10") 140p, 386 illus. c. 1977. Covers 739cc, all models, 1971 to c. 1977.

Suzuki 50 M30 Workshop Manual 1964-67. c. 1968.

Suzuki 50 and 80 Handbook 1964-67. Pitman, c. 1968.

Suzuki T10/T20/T200 1964-68.

Suzuki 200/250 T10/T20/T200 Workshop Manual, 1964-68. Los Angeles: Cloyd Clymer, c. 1969.

Suzuki Singles. softbound 17.8 x 25.4 cm (7 x 10") 166p, 300 illus. Los Angeles: Clymer, c. 1986.

Suzuki RM50-400 Twin Shock Singles. softbound 17.8 x. 25.4 cm (7 x 10") 219p, 545 illus. Los Angeles: Clymer, c. 1986. Covers 1975-81.

Suzuki DS80-250 Singles. softbound 17.8 x 25.4 cm (7 x 10") 133p, 383 illus. Los Angeles: Clymer, c. 1986. Covers 1978-80.

Suzuki PE175-400 Singles. softbound 17.8 x 25.4 cm (7 x 10") 191p, 526 illus. Los Angeles: Clymer, c. 1986. Covers 1977-81.

Suzuki Singles. softbound 17.8 x 25.4 cm (7 x 10") 130p, 235 illus. Los Angeles: Clymer, c. 1986. Covers 125-400cc, 1964-81.

Suzuki Twins. softbound 17.8 x 25.4 cm (7 x 10") 149p, 354 illus. Los Angeles: Clymer, c. 1986. Covers 125-500cc, 1964-76.

Suzuki GS400-450 Twins. softbound 17.8 x 25.4 cm (7 x 10") 265p, 480 illus. Los Angeles: Clymer, c. 1986. Covers 1977-83.

Suzuki Triples. softbound 17.8 x 25.4 cm (7 x 10") 165p, 274 illus. Los Angeles: Clymer, c. 1986. Covers 380-750cc, 1972-77.

Suzuki GS550 Fours. softbound 17.8 x 25.4 cm (7 x 10") 169p, 512 illus. Los Angeles: Clymer, c. 1986. Covers 1977-83.

Suzuki GS750 Fours. softbound 17.8 x 25.4 cm (7 x 10") 340p, 615 illus. Los Angeles: Clymer, c. 1986. Covers 1977-82.

Suzuki GS750 Fours 1981-83. softbound 17.8 x 25.4 cm (7 x 10") 303p, 857 illus. Los Angeles: Clymer, c. 1986.

Suzuki GS850 and GS1000 Shaft Drive Fours. softbound 17.8 x 25.4 cm (7 x 10") 191p, 549 illus. Los Angeles: Clymer, c. 1986. Covers 1979-84.

Suzuki GS ang GSX1100 Fours. softbound 17.8 x 25.4 cm (7 x 10") Los Angeles: Clymer, c. 1986. Covers 1980-81.

Thorpe, John. Suzuki. 50 and 80cc models.

TRIUMPH (British)

Bacon, Roy. Triumph Singles. 218p, 100 illus. Osprey Collector's Library, c. 1986. Covers late prewar models including Terrier, Cub, Trophy, Blazer and scooters.

_____. Triumph Twin Restoration. hardbound $7\frac{1}{4}$ x 11" 240p, 200 illus. 1985. Pre-1972 production twins.

_____. Triumph Twins and Triples. hardbound $7\frac{1}{2}$ x $8\frac{1}{2}$" 192p, 165 illus. c. 1986. Covers 350, 500, 650 and 750 Twins and Trident.

BSA, Sunbeam and Triumph Tigress Handbook. Pitman, c. 1969.

Chilton's Triumph Motorcycle Repair and Tune-up Guide. softbound, 17.8 x 26.1 cm (7 x 10¼") 201p, 260 illus. c. 1977. Covers unit-construction 250, 500, 650 and 750 models through 1972.

Clymer Triumph Service, Repair Handbook. softbound 17.8 x 25.4 cm (7 x 10") 234p, 265 illus. c. 1977. Covers 500-750cc twins, 1963-76.

Clymer Triumph Service, Repair Handbook. softbound 17.8 x 25.4 cm (7 x 10") 246p, 311 illus. Los Angeles: Clymer, c. 1977. Covers Twins 500-750cc 1963-1979.

The First Classic Triumph Scene. 64p, 123 illus. c. 1986. Begins with pre-war coverage.

Glenn, Harold T. Glenn's Triumph. 34p. New York: c. 1971.

Haynes Triumph 350/500 Unit Twins Owner's Workshop Manual. softbound 27.3 x 21 cm (10-3/4 x 8¼") 159p, 232 illus. c. 1977. Covers 349, 490cc, 1958 to c. 1977.

Haynes Triumph 650 and 750 Twins Owner's Workshop Manual. softbound 27.3 x 21 cm (10-3/4 x 8¼") 150p, 240 illus. c. 1977. Covers unit construction 649 and 747cc, 1963 to c. 1977.

Haynes Triumph Trident Owner's Workshop Manual. softbound 27.3 x 21 cm (10-3/4 x 8¼") 132 p, 250 illus. c. 1977. Covers BSA Rocket 3, 741cc, 1969 to c. 1977.

Haynes Triumph Pre-unit Twins Owner's Workshop Manual. softbound 27.3 x 21 cm (10-3/4 x 8¼") 112p, 213 illus. c. 1977. Covers all models 1947-62.

Haycraft. Triumph Twins. Models 1956-67, except T100T, and T120R.

Louis, Harry and Bob Corrie. The Story of Triumph Motorcycles. hardbound 128p, 90 photographs. c. 1977. History to 1973 and the formation of Norton Villiers Triumph.

Masters, A. St.J. Triumph Owners Handbook. 1937 through 1951. 216p, 100 illus. Los Angeles: Clymer Publications. Repair, maintenance, and mechanical and electrical factory specifications on all models for the period.

Nelson, J.R. Bonnie. The Development History of the Triumph Bonneville. softbound 165p, 129 illus. c. 1986.

Nelson, John. Triumph Bonneville Super Profile. 56p, 87 illus, 20 in color. c. 1986.

Shenton, Stan. Triumph Speed Tuning. 64p, 88 illus. 1982.

130 / Motorcycle Books

Triumph Motorcycle Operation and Care Manual 1946-1947. 66p, 27 illus. Reprint of factory manual, c. 1986.

Triumph Motorcycles Pictorial History. hardbound 10 x 7½" 96p, 160 illus. c. 1985.

Triumph Parts Catalogue. 81p, 75 illus. c. 1986. Covers the 1972 Bonneville T120R, T120RV, Tiger 650 TR6R and TR6RV, Trophy 650 TR6C, Tr6CV, and 1974 Bonneville 750 and Tiger 750.

Triumph Pre-unit Twins. 112p. Haynes, c. 1986. Covers all models 1947-62.

Triumph: Service-Repair Handbook, 500cc and 650cc Twins, 1963-1971. 214p. Los Angeles: Clymer, c. 1972.

Triumph Singles Maintenance and Repair Manual, 1937-61. Pearson, c. 1969.

Triumph 150 and 200 Singles Workshop Instruction Manual 1953-62. Pearson, c. 1968.

1937 Triumph Tiger 70, 80, 90 and DeLuxe Owner's Manual. 4½ x 7½" 19p, 12 illus. c. 1986.

Triumph Tiger Cub and Terrier. 111p. Haynes, c. 1986. Covers 149 and 199cc, 1952-1968.

Triumph 500 and 650 Twins Workshop Instruction Manual 1945-55. 216p, 90 charts, photographs and drawings. Los Angeles: Clymer, c. 1968.

Triumph Twins Handbook 1945-67. Pitman. c. 1968.

Triumph Twins Handbook 1956-67. Pitman, c. 1969.

Triumph 350 and 500 Twins Workshop Instruction Manual 1958-63. c. 1968.

Triumph 350/500 Twins Workshop Manual 1963-67. c. 1968.

Triumph 350/500 Twins 1964-68. c. 1969.

Triumph 650 Twins Workshop Manual 1964-69. c. 1968.

Triumph Twins. 246p, 311 illus. Los Angeles: Clymer, c. 1986. Covers 500-750cc, 1963-79.

VELOCETTE (British)

Bacon, Roy. Velocette: The Little Twins. hardbound 7¼ x 8½" 128p, 100 illus. 1985. Covers models LE, Valient, Viceroy and Vogue.

Burgess, R.W. Always in the Picture: A History of the Velocette Motorcycle. hardbound 7¼ x 10" 285p, 167 illus. 1971. History from 1860 through this century. Revised c. 1986.

Burris, Rod. Velocette: A Development History of the MSS, Venom, Viper, Truxton and Scrambler Models. 139 illus. c. 1986. Covers mid-fifties to 1971.

Haynes Velocette Singles Owner's Workshop Manual. softbound 27.3 x 21 cm (10-3/4 x 8¼") 136p, 262 illus. c. 1977. Covers 349 and 499cc, 1953-71.

Main-Smith, Bruce. The First Velocette Scene. 64p, 123 photographs. Published by Bruce Main-Smith, c. 1977. Covers mid-seventies survivors.

———. Velocette Motorcycles 1925 to 1952. 62p, 30 illus. Published by Bruce Main-Smith, c. 1977. Workshop manual for all single-cylinder K-M-GTP roadsters and 148 and 192 LE twins.

Masters, Dave. Velocette 1905 to 1971: An Illustrated Reference. hardbound 192p, 90 illus. c. 1977.

Moseley, Leonard J. My Velocette Days. 120p, 49 photographs. c. 1977. 1923 to 1970 at the Veloce factories.

Velocette All Models Maintenance Manual 1925-52. Temple Press, c. 1969.

Velocette All Models 1925-66. c. 1968.

Velocette All Models Handbook 1925-68. Pitman, c. 1969.

VILLIERS (British)

Bacon, Roy. Villiers Singles and Twins. 192p, 165 illus. Osprey Collector's Library, c. 1986.

Browning, B.E. Villiers Maintenance and Repair Manual 1949-60. c. 1969.

Grange. Villiers. Models up to 1963.

Villiers All Models Maintenance Manual 1935-55. Temple Press, c. 1969.

132 / Motorcycle Books

Villiers Engines 1935-55. Motor Cycling (Magazine), c. 1969.

Villiers Engines 1949-60. Pearson, c. 1968.

Villiers Engines Handbook 1953-67. Pitman, c. 1968. Also: 1953-69.

Villiers Engines: Maintenance and Parts Catalog. 40p, 56 illus. c. 1986. Covers the 31C, 2L, 3L, 9E, 10E, 11E, 31A, 32A, 33A, 34A, 36A and 37A.

1949 Villiers Mk. 10D and Mk. 6# Owner's Manual. 5½ x 8¼" 27p, 11 illus. c. 1986.

Villiers Mark 4T Twins Workshop Manual 1962-68. c. 1969.

Villiers 150-250 Singles Workshop Manual 1955-70. Villiers, c. 1970.

Villiers Singles Workshop Manual 1955-68. Villiers, c. 1969.

Villiers 250 Twins Workshop Manual 1962-69. c. 1970.

1925 Villiers Two-Stroke Owner's Manual. 5 x 8" 24p, 29 illus. c. 1986.

VINCENT (British)

Bickerstaff, Peter. Vincent Twins. 56p, 90 illus, 20 in color. c. 1986. History, specifications, purchasing and clubs.

Carrick, Peter. Vincent-HRD. 88p, 134 illus. World Motorcycle Series, c. 1986.

Harper, Roy. Vincent H.R.D. Gallery. 75p, 75 illus. c. 1977. Covers entire productions of Howard Davies and Philip Vincent.

_____. The Vincent HRD Story. 220p, 98 illus. Bruce Main-Smith, c. 1986.

_____. Vincent Vee Twins. 190p, 180 illus. Osprey Collector's Library, c. 1986. Covers the 1000 series and the 500 singles.

Main-Smith, Bruce. The First Vincent-HRD Scene. 64p, 109 illus. Published by Bruce Main-Smith, c. 1977.

_____. Vincent H.R.D. 500/1000 Motorcycles 1947-55. 60p, 29 illus. Published by Bruce Main-Smith. Also: Motor Cycling (Magazine), Temple Press, c. 1969. Singles and twins troubleshooting and performance.

Richardson, Paul. Vincent Owner's Handbook: 1935 through 1955.

216p, 124 photographs, charts and drawings. Los Angeles: Clymer, c. 1969. Also: Vincent Maintenance and Repair Manual 1935-55. c. 1969.

Stevens, E.M.G. Know Thy Beast--A Book for the Vincent Rider. 194p, 24 illus. c. 1986.

Vincent Maintenance and Repair Manual 1935-55. Pearson, c. 1968. Also: Los Angeles: Clymer, c. 1970. All models.

YAMAHA (Japanese)

Chilton's Yamaha Four-Stroke Repair and Tune-up Guide. softbound 17.8 x 26.1 cm (7 x 10¼") 155p, 485 illus. c. 1977. Covers all 500 and 750 four-stroke models from 1970 to 1974.

Chilton's Yamaha Enduros Repair and Tune-up Guide. softbound 17.8 x 26.1 cm (7 x 10¼") 190p, 340 illus. c. 1977. Covers Enduro, Trail and MX models, 1968-74.

Chilton's Yamaha Street Two-Strokes Repair and Tune-up Guide. softbound 17.8 x 26.1 cm (7 x 10¼") 199p, 400 illus. c. 1977. Covers single and twin-cylinder models, 1967-75.

Clymer Yamaha Service, Repair Handbook. softbound 17.8 x 25.4 cm (7 x 10") 192p, 290 illus. c. 1977. Covers 80-175cc Enduro and Motocross, 1968-76.

_____. softbound 17.8 x 25.4 cm (7 x 10") 198p, 335 illus. c. 1977. Covers 250-500cc Enduro and Motocross, 1968-77.

_____. softbound 17.8 x 25.4 cm (7 x 10") 199p, 395 illus. c. 1977. Covers 650cc twins, 1970-76.

_____. softbound 17.8 x 25.4 cm (7 x 10") 140p, 260 illus. c. 1977. Covers rotary valve singles, 1963-76.

_____. softbound 17.8 x 25.4 cm (7 x 10") 12p, 163 illus. c. 1977. Covers 90-200cc twins, 1966-75.

Clymer Yamaha XS360 Service, Repair Handbook. c. 1977. Covers 1976-77.

Clymer Yamaha Twins Service, Repair Handbook. c. 1977. Covers 250, 350cc, 1965-77.

Clymer Yamaha Service, Repair Handbook. Yamaha Piston-port Singles. softbound 17.8 x 25.4 cm (7 x 10") 184p, 321 illus. c. 1986. Covers 250-400cc, 1968-76.

_____. Yamaha XJ550 Fours 1981-1983. softbound 17.8 x 25.4 cm (7 x 10") 240p, 434 illus. c. 1986.

_____. Yamaha XT500 and TT500 Singles. softbound 17.8 x 25.4 cm (7 x 10") 196p, 355 illus. c. 1986. Covers 1976-1981.

_____. Yamaha YZ50-80 Monoshock Singles. softbound 17.8 x 25.4 cm (7 x 10") 292p, 529 illus. c. 1986. Covers 1978-1982.

_____. Yamaha YZ100-490 Monoshock Singles. softbound 17.8 x 25.4 cm (7 x 10") 345 p, 624 illus. c. 1986. Covers 1976-84.

_____. Yamaha DT and MX Singles. softbound 17.8 x 25.4 cm (7 x 10") 305p, 552 illus. c. 1986. Covers 1977-83.

_____. Yamaha IT125-425 Singles. softbound 17.8 x 25.4 cm (7 x 10") 341p, 617 illus. c. 1986. Covers 1976-83.

_____. Yamaha SR500 Singles. softbound 17.8 x 25.4 cm (7 x 10") 201p, 564 illus. c. 1986. Covers 1977-80.

_____. Yamaha Twins. softbound 17.8 x 25.4 cm (7 x 10") 200p, 262 illus. c. 1986. Covers 250-400cc, 1965-79.

_____. Yamaha Twins. softbound 17.8 x 25.4 cm (7 x 10") 221p, 400 illus. c. 1986. Covers 650cc, 1970-81.

_____. Yamaha XS750 and 850 Triplets. softbound 17.8 x 25.4 cm (7 x 10") 259p, 644 illus. c. 1986. Covers 1976-81.

_____. Yamaha XS1100 Fours. softbound 17.8 x 25.4 cm (7 x 10") 268p, 749 illus. c. 1986. Covers 1978-81.

Haynes Yamaha Trail Bikes Owner's Workshop Manual. softbound 27.3 x 21 cm (10-3/4 x 8¼") 115p, 241 illus. c. 1977. Covers 97, 123 and 171cc, 1971 to c. 1977.

Haynes Yamaha 200 Twins Owner's Workshop Manual. softbound 27.3 x 21 cm (10-3/4 x 8¼") 100p, 164 illus. c. 1977. Covers YCS3E and YCS5E Electric, RD200, 195cc 1971 to c. 1977.

Haynes Yamaha 250 and 350 Twins Owner's Workshop Manual. softbound 27.3 c 21 cm (10-3/4 x 8¼") 119p, 255 illus. c. 1977. Covers 247 and 347cc, 1970 to c. 1977.

Haynes Yamaha RD 400 Twin Owner's Workshop Manual. softbound 27.3 x 21 cm (10-3/4 x 8¼") 119p, 265 illus. c. 1977. Covers 398cc, all models 1975 to c. 1977.

Haynes Yamaha Trail Bikes 250, 360 and 400 Owner's Workshop Manual. softbound 27.3 x 21 cm (10-3/4 x 8¼") 111p, 220 illus. c. 1977. Covers 246, 351 and 397cc, 1971 to c. 1977.

Haynes Yamaha 500 Twin Owner's Workshop Manual. softbound 27.3 x 21 cm (10-3/4 x 8¼") 139p, 345 illus. c. 1977. Covers TX and XS 500 series, 1973 to c. 1977.

Haynes Yamaha 650 Twins. softbound 27.3 x 21 cm (10-3/4 x 8¼") 175p, 420 illus. c. 1986. Covers 654cc, all models, 1970-80.

Haynes Yamaha XV750, XV920 and TR1V. softbound 27.3 x 21 cm (10-3/4 x 8¼") 279p, 400 illus. c. 1986.

Macauley, Ted. Yamaha. hardbound 7 x 9½" 283p, 170 illus. 1979. Originally titled <u>Yamaha Legend</u>; updated through 1983 under this title, above.

Mackellar, Colin. Yamaha Two-Stroke Twins. hardbound 7½ x 8½" 192p, 160 illus. Osprey Collector's Library, c. 1986. History 1956 to c. 1986.

Woollett, Mick. Yamaha. 64p, 36 color photographs. c. 1986. History.

Yamaha. c. 1969. Most models 1963-68.

ZUNDAPP (German)

Zundapp Repair-Work on the Twostroke Engine (50-75cc Models). c. 1968.

Zundapp Repair-Work on the Twostroke Engine (150-250cc Models) 1951-63. c. 1968.

ABOUT THE COMPILER

Kirby Congdon has written reviews and a short story for <u>Motorcyclist</u> magazine, and two books--poems entitled <u>Dream-Work</u> (1970) (called "an underground classic" by the Canadian bibliographer and poet Ian Young, and reprinted in Wales) and prose poems, <u>Fantoccini</u> (1981)--that center on the mystique of motorcycling and motorcyclists.

Congdon compiled <u>Contemporary Poets in American Anthologies 1960-1977</u> for Scarecrow Press in 1978. A book collector, he started this survey on motorcycle books when the literature on the subject began to accumulate with the postwar motorcycle boom in the United States. An anthology of motorcycle poems is in progress, which he compiled during his research on motorcycle books.